Needless Casualties of War

Endorsements

Limping Christians, millions of them. They took aim at Satan and shot themselves in the foot. If you are one of them, or don't wish to be, read John Paul Jackson's *Needless Casualties of War*, my favorite manual on spiritual warfare.

Harald Bredesen
Chairman, The Prince of Peace Foundation

I read this exciting book in one sitting. John Paul Jackson has done us all a great service in addressing spiritual warfare with his God-inspired revelation and his well-earned common sense. Loaded with real-life stories and anchored in a theology forged through experience, this book will fascinate you as it teaches you. You *gotta* read this book!

Wesley Campbell
Pastor, New Life Vineyard, Kelowna, Canada
Director, Revival Now! Ministries

In *Needless Casualties of War*, the Holy Spirit has given John Paul Jackson clarity, revelation, and insight for the Church. I read this book in one sitting. I hope it engages your spirit as it did mine.

Dr. Guy Chevreau
Itinerant and Author of *Catch the Fire*

In *Needless Casualties of War*, John Paul Jackson exposes the dangers of addressing Satan in warfare prayer while providing us with biblical incentive to enthrone Christ and so battle wisely and well. An *invaluable* tool for all who prayerfully seek to overcome evil with good.

Rev. Andrew Comiskey
Founder and Director, Desert Stream Ministries
Pastor, Vineyard Christian Fellowship, Anaheim, California

Needless Casualties of War presents a revolutionary perspective that has the potential to change the Church's understanding of spiritual warfare forever. John Paul Jackson offers a theology of warfare that is so simple, yet so profound. This book is a must-read on spiritual warfare for all leaders in the Church. Now we can pursue the victory within our proper spiritual authority.

Dr. J. Patrick Fiore
Pastor, C.Net USA, West Milford, New Jersey

Needless Casualties of War will super-charge your faith! With great wisdom, John Paul Jackson reveals the simplicity and authority of spiritual warfare when our focus is on God and His purposes, not on the schemes of the enemy.

Olen Griffing
Senior Pastor, Shady Grove Church, Dallas, Texas

Tragically, the topic of spiritual warfare has caused tremendous division within the Church. In this profoundly insightful and exciting book, John Paul Jackson clears the smoke by focusing on solid biblical teaching. I am convinced this book can join the hearts of evangelicals and charismatics in fulfilling the Great Commission.

Kenn Gulliksen
Pastor, Sojourners Church, Los Angeles, California

John Paul Jackson is a man of God with great humility and keen vision. We need such servants who will bring us back to the plumbline. I recommend this book to anyone who desires success in spiritual warfare. It will cause you to become a channel for the release of God's power—for revival, restoration, and impact!

Davis L. Hill
Pastor, Gateway Church, Brea, California

Four years ago, I became a needless casualty of war. I wish I had known then the foundational principles of this outstanding book. Anyone who engages the evil one in warfare needs to read this book carefully and prayerfully. It will offer immediate and immense help. This book will change the rest of your life.

Dr. Kregg Hood
Founder, Full Message Ministries

This is not *just* another book on spiritual warfare. John Paul Jackson has given the Body of Christ a serious look at many areas of spiritual warfare that often go ignored or are abused. His balanced and yet radical approach to cutting-edge Christian faith is a breath of fresh air. This book is an essential manual for all serious warriors!

Don James
Senior Pastor, Bethany Assembly of God, Wyckoff, New Jersey

Needless Casualties of War brings great wisdom to the task of spiritual warfare and gives us clear direction on how to do spiritual warfare without opening us up to unnecessary attack. I highly recommend this book to pastors and intercessors.

Dr. Daniel Juster
Director, Tikkun Ministries

This long overdue book, so lovingly written, should lead people away from a wrong focus and help them to engage in a spiritual warfare that is biblical.

Dr. R. T. Kendall
Pastor, Westminster Chapel, London, England

John Paul Jackson has written a vitally important book. Born out of personal experience, revelation and thoughtful reflection, *Needless Casualties of War* contributes valuable insights to spiritual warfare. Every intercessor and every pastor involved in city-reaching should read this book.

Rick McKinniss
Pastor, Kensington Baptist Church, Kensington, Connecticut

Needless Casualties of War is a masterpiece like a word fitly spoken. Filled with godly wisdom, this book is biblically anchored and seasoned through years of practical teaching. This book is necessary reading for Christians who want victory over the evil one.

Ras Robinson
President, Fullness in Christ Ministries

In *Needless Casualties of War*, you will discover foundational truths that will help you walk in the power and anointing of the Lord. John Paul Jackson provides a wealth of insight into what it takes to be a successful spiritual warrior today.

James Ryle
Founder and President, TruthWorks Ministry

John Paul Jackson's book will spare many of us the heartache of being wounded in action. Read this book from cover-to-cover and stand complete in Jesus Christ with a new understanding of spiritual warfare principles.

Brian Simmons
Pastor, Gateway Christian Fellowship, West Haven, Connecticut

This revelation given to John Paul Jackson offers a loving protection for all who will heed its wisdom. It provides safe boundaries for our weapons of war and reveals how to use the keys of the Kingdom without presumption. *Needless Casualties of War* places our focus where it should be: on Jesus, Who modeled true spiritual authority on the Earth!

Sandy Warner
Intercessor and Founder, The Quickened Word

John Paul Jackson is kind, though clear, in his admonitions to intercessors to stay on the road that Jesus, His apostles, and followers walked in dealing with demonic forces. The Church would greatly benefit to heed John Paul's encouragement to use the weapons of warfare that Jesus gave us.

Carol Wimber
widow of the late John Wimber, Founder of the Vineyard Movement International

John Paul Jackson

Needless Casualties of War

Streams
MINISTRIES INTERNATIONAL
™

To the hundreds of intercessors
who had the courage to share their stories,
may your fervor for prayer grow and propel the glorious
Kingdom of God so that it covers the Earth as the water
covers the sea. Nothing happens without you! For you take
the desires of God and ask Him to accomplish His will
on the Earth as it is in Heaven. For it is from Him,
to Him and through Him that all things exist.

To my loving wife Diane,
who has stood by me as I sought the Lord concerning this
topic. Her unwavering support has proved true the divine
compassion behind God's reasoning in creating a woman
and a man. I would not be complete without her.

In memory of the late John Wimber,
former pastor of the Vineyard Christian Fellowship in
Anaheim, California, and founder of the Vineyard
Movement International, who recognized God's hand in
my life, loved to hear God's revelation, and encouraged me
to write this book. Years ago, he advised me to wait
until I was "closer to 50 and more seasoned" to write it.
In heeding his wisdom, I waited.

Foreword

I REGARD IT a privilege and an honor to write this foreword for John Paul Jackson's book, *Needless Casualties of War*. Not merely because I hold John Paul in high esteem, but because I believe this is a rare commodity in these prolific days of book writing—one commanded by God, inspired by the Holy Spirit, and desperately needed in the Body of Christ. Many possess one or the other, but few possess all three.

As John Paul states in the preface, engaging in spiritual warfare has become increasingly popular. Many are leaping in response to the call of God, eager to serve as soldiers. This is good. If I thought that this book was in any way an attack upon spiritual warfare, or on those of us involved in it, I could not write even an endorsement, much less a foreword. I am myself greatly engaged in spiritual warfare, and many of those most known for it are some of my dearest friends.

Historically, when we in the Charismatic movement first discovered that demons were real, we rushed into the fray inexperienced, and in many ways ignorant and naïve. We blundered along, learning as we went—and the cause of Christ suffered a number of casualties. It has been the same in nearly every area in which the Holy Spirit has been rediscovering to us His ancient paths in which to walk (Isaiah 58:12)—for example: the speaking in tongues, the giving of prophetic words, or the Faith movement. The pendulum swings to zeal, mistakes, embarrassments, and repentance, and then to the far side in reaction—rejection, avoidance, harsh criticisms, and retrenching in the old ways that maybe didn't work, but at least gave us a sense of security by being familiar. We felt in control again. After several swings, usually we settle into balance and find wisdom, and learn to serve appropriately, eventually even restfully, at ease in what is no longer threateningly new.

I don't suppose there is much possibility of avoiding such a history in any newly rediscovered area, nor perhaps should there be. Pearls are a symbol of wisdom because an irritant gets inside an oyster's shell and it has to work to weave a covering around it. There may be no other or better way to gain wisdom than by "the school of hard knocks." Our loving heavenly Father knew this, and from before creation He purposed to pay the price for our freedom to bumble and sin and learn. He knew that the cost for raising sons and daughters mature enough to give Him adult fellowship, person-to-Person, would have to be His own suffering through the death of His only begotten Son on the Cross.

Therefore, there should be no shame or condemnation laid upon us when we stumble into new fields, swinging to revulsion and back again, eventually to find balance and wisdom.

Since the Charismatic movement has grown more mature rather rapidly in recent years, we may have entered into spiritual warfare with much less of the usual foolish mistakes and wild pendulum swings. I have witnessed remarkable maturity already for such a newly begotten movement. But I have also observed some mistakes, sins, and consequent sufferings.

Therefore, there have been a number of needless casualties. *Needless* means "without unnecessary risks and harms had we been operating in the fullness of experience and hard-won wisdom," not needless in the sense of, "Shame on you. You should have known better." It is to aid the swing of the pendulum to the safer realms of wisdom that John Paul has written this book. The Holy Spirit has put into his heart great love and concern for all of us involved in spiritual warfare and laid upon him a burden of prayer and intercession for the entire field, that it not fail to accomplish the purposes for which God has called us to become His army for this critical time.

To that end, I believe God has mandated that John Paul run the risks of writing a book containing many suggested corrections in the way we think and act in spiritual warfare. Our fleshly nature being what it is, reproofs and instructions are seldom popular. But we are trusting that the risks of misunderstandings—and rejections because some do understand and don't want to hear—will be lessened by the grace of God and the increased level of maturity in the Body of Christ.

Proverbs 9:8-9 says that if you rebuke a wise man, he will love you for it, and if you give instruction to a man of wisdom, he will become the wiser for it. We believe there is, at present, maturity in the Body and a hunger for counsel and instruction, so that we can conduct warfare without needless casualties.

The unique element in this case is that in many other fields, we could blunder and mature by trial and error without much danger. Learning to do exorcisms did involve some risk, and some Christians did get hurt, but that was minor compared to the risks and injuries that can occur in spiritual warfare. That is what makes this book so timely and crucial. The longer it takes to receive instruction and gain wisdom, the more people can be potentially wounded.

Readers will find in these pages warnings, definitions, distinctions, clarifications, teachings as to how to conduct spiritual warfare with minimal risk, and practical suggestions for maintaining personal health and freedom from defilement while engaged in warfare. Any one of these alone would be worth the effort of reading. The keys of knowledge presented here may save your own life much harm or even death, as well as perhaps your relatives, friends, and church community.

I believe this book is a *must* for any who would enter the Lord's army for the battles that are here, and the ones to come, as the climax of history draws ever nearer.

John A. Sandford
Founder, Elijah House Ministries

Contents

Acknowledgments

As we walk out the tapestry of our lives, God brings us in contact with many people who help determine its eventual beauty. Without the threads of many lives weaving around and about us, the tapestry would be formless and tattered. There would be no beauty, contrast, direction, or tonality. But worst of all, there would be no one to love and be loved by.

In eternity, when we gaze at the tapestry God designed, we will be surprised whose thread crossed ours and thus changed our lives. Conversely, those who touched our lives were also changed, and their change in turn changed others.

Eventually, our tapestry is comprised by those who even indirectly touched our lives, though generations away. Yet, God sees that their legacy is woven into our tapestry much to His great delight.

Sometimes when we are first pierced by a person's impact upon us, change is hardly noticed. Often years transpire before the change is evident. Sadly, by then, we may have forgotten the essence of the moment and perhaps even the name of the person from whom change began.

Acknowledgements may therefore be a weak attempt of trying to recover initial moments that led us to the weaving of this particular piece of our tapestry. It would be a futile attempt to try to recognize all those who have helped to weave the pages of this book. Except to say, only the Lord in His infinite wisdom could weave any of our tapestries together to comprise the beautiful tapestry of the Kingdom.

I would like to thank those who have closer proximity to accomplishing this moment:

To Carolyn Blunk who took my clumsy attempts, notes, and tapes and turned them into a manuscript, I am awestruck. My gratitude also goes to Randa Rottschafer, Michael Giobbe and Don and Sandy Rice for research assistance, to Ed Tuttle for his dazzling designs, and to friends who reviewed and critiqued the manuscript.

To the team at Streams Ministries, I am grateful for your endurance as you continue to work tirelessly to implement the vision the Lord has given me. I am humbled by your servant hearts. My heartfelt gratitude also goes to intercessors around the country who prayed while the book was being written.

And finally to John Sandford, who has been an invaluable source of wisdom, understanding, rebuke, and courage over the years, and who has stood up and covered me with his prophetic wings when I needed it most, I am eternally grateful. Thank you for your friendship.

Preface

COUNTLESS NUMBERS of Christians are rediscovering spiritual warfare. Bookshelves are stocked with bestsellers about battling unseen spiritual forces in the heavenly realms. And seminars on the cosmic dimensions of warfare are proliferating around the globe.

Yet spiritual warfare remains one of the most controversial subjects in the Church today. Some people believe that Christians should not wrestle with demonic spirits in the Heavens. Others believe that everyone should bind demonic principalities and powers in Heaven as well as on the Earth. Still others believe that only a select few—high ranking intercessors—are anointed to bind demonic spirits that rule over geographic areas of the world.

Several years ago, I embraced much of the popular teaching on spiritual warfare. Like my peers, I believed that spiritual warfare would change the destiny of cities and nations. I still do.

In recent years, however, I have adopted a more conservative perspective on spiritual warfare—one that allows me to distinguish between warfare in a terrestrial arena from warfare in the second Heaven arena. It is my belief that unless you understand the parameters of our delegated authority and some practical guidelines on how to properly engage in spiritual warfare, there's a strong possibility that you could become an unfortunate victim of war.

I have written this book to share some insights and to offer a word of discernment. I do so humbly, because I do not wish to imply that I have *all* the answers on spiritual warfare. I do not. But I will attempt to explain why I have embraced a different perspective, in the hope that you will avoid the unnecessary heartache that has befallen many intercessors over the years.

It's my prayer that you will have a greater understanding how to protect yourself, your family, and your church from the unforeseen and unperceived spiritual attacks that have afflicted so many believers.

The Heaven, even the Heavens, are the Lord's;
but the Earth He has given to the children of men.

–PSALM 115:16

There is a way that seems right to a man,
but its end is the way of death.

–PROVERBS 16:25

Chapter One

A Dark Cloud

I LISTENED QUIETLY to the story unfolding on the other end of the line. The caller was desperate. Holding the receiver to my ear, I began to scribble notes on a pad of paper as the pastor of a large, rapidly-growing congregation explained his problem.

In the past year, five women at his church had miscarried babies and now three more women looked as if they were going to lose their pregnancies. "What in the world is going on?" he asked. "Is there a curse on me or my church?" After we talked for a while, I promised that I would pray and seek God for some answers.

As part of the pastoral staff of a large church in Anaheim, California, it was not uncommon for me to receive phone calls from leaders around the world. God would often give me words of knowledge and revelatory insight into demonic oppression and various spiritual enigmas in order to unlock troubling situations.

While I was speaking at a conference on the East Coast a few days later, a woman approached me asking for prayer. With tears in her eyes, she explained that she was pregnant and recently showed signs of miscarrying. Her three prior pregnancies had also been lost prematurely through miscarriages. Although she was 42-years-old, she did not believe her inability to have children was due to her age. Her daughter, who was pregnant, was also showing signs of losing her unborn child. She bit her lip, trying to control her emotions, but tears streamed down her face. Hearing her cry for help, I rested my hand on her head and began to pray for her and her family.

As the crowd pressed forward for prayer, a pastor threaded his way to the front with a woman at his side. When our eyes made contact, he pleaded for me to pray for one of his leaders. "She is the head intercessor in our church," he said protectively. "Satan has really been attacking her. She lost two pregnancies through miscarriages."

I was suddenly intrigued and wondered if a connection existed with the previous woman's story. As I prayed for this woman, I asked God for clearer revelation about the dark cloud that was suspiciously hanging over so many intercessors. Unable at the moment to put my finger on what it was, I knew that God would unravel the mystery.

Soon after I returned to the West Coast, a pastor called my office. With great distress, he explained that his 16-year-old son had run away from home. "My son has always been godly," he said quietly, "until last year. He dyed his hair purple, pierced his ears, shaved one side of his head, and tattooed his body. I can't understand what happened."

Greatly perplexed, the pastor seemed at the end of his rope. I told him I was sorry about his son and promised to pray for him. Exchanging phone numbers, we agreed to stay in touch.

Another pastor who was deeply shaken called me. His college-aged daughter had become gravely and mysteriously ill. Her condition worsened daily until she became bedridden and had to withdraw from school. Diagnosed with chronic fatigue syndrome and fibromyalgia, she had to be placed under a doctor's care.

Over the ensuing weeks and months, similar phone calls came. Some from church leaders whose spouses had left. Others called to describe sudden illnesses and operations; one intercessor developed cancer, and a young couple lost their newborn baby. Each situation seemed to arrive with little forewarning and created devastating results.

Puzzled by these heart-wrenching stories, I was deeply stirred in my spirit. Alone with God, I began to ask for revelation. Although I had been praying for greater insight into spiritual warfare, I was unaware of any connection. Little did I know that these circumstances had a common thread woven together into a tapestry of unnecessary sorrow, heartbreak, and tragedy.

Chapter Two

A Deadly Trap

THROUGHOUT THE BIBLE, God has used dreams to give guidance, direction, and warning. Those who obeyed these messages were often spared from famine, disease, and death.

Even today, God visits us through dreams and gives us solutions to what we have been seeking. Just as God spoke to Daniel in a dream, God used a dream to change my understanding of spiritual warfare forever and to prevent some of the heartbreaking tragedies that have plagued so many Christians.

Living in Anaheim, California, I had been petitioning God about spiritual warfare. One night, God spoke to me in a dream. During the dream, I watched its drama unfold as if I were suspended in the sky.

Throwing Hatchets at the Moon

It was night, the sky was blue-black except for a huge luminous moon that filled the horizon. In the remote blackness, several figures were silhouetted against the moon. Each figure stood on a circular platform and preached to a small group of people.

With great emotion, these leaders pointed and shouted at the moon, urging others to follow them. Gradually, each leader's platform rose higher as the crowds grew larger. Some platforms rose above the crowds to precarious heights. Others lifted only slightly off the ground.

Resembling gunslingers, the leaders stood on the platforms with holsters strapped to their hips. But instead of guns in the holsters, there were hatchets tucked inside. As the leaders began to preach, crowds of people gathered around them. Then, each leader grabbed a hatchet, waved it around, and hurled it at the moon. But the hatchet never hit the moon; it simply fell into the darkness that lay beyond.

After some time, the leaders grew weary. Eventually, each lay down on his or her platform and fell asleep. Then with undetected stealth, several dark figures dropped off the moon's surface. They crawled up poles which held up the platforms, sneaked over, and began to attack the leaders with extreme viciousness.

Since the platforms were large and lofty, no one had been alerted to the coming devastation. Soon, blood-curdling cries came forth from the leaders—cries for their families, their children, their churches, and their ministries.

"Somebody help me, I'm dying," someone pleaded. It was a terrifying sight and sound. Then, the dream faded to black. In the stillness that followed, God spoke to me:

> To attack principalities and powers over a geographic area can be as useless as throwing hatchets at the moon. And it can leave you open to unforeseen and unperceived attacks.

God's words echoed in my mind. These leaders did not foresee principalities counterattacking them. They believed they were doing something great for God. They failed to comprehend the nature of the enemy's authority to retaliate with fierceness.

God's Sovereignty as Judge

Then, I heard the voice of God declare two passages of Scripture:

> In that day the Lord with His severe sword, great and strong, will punish Leviathan the fleeing serpent. Leviathan that twisted serpent; and He will slay the reptile that is in the sea.
>
> –Isaiah 27:1

In this passage, Leviathan is a metaphor for Satan. As such, he is pictured as a fleeing serpent which refers to God revoking Satan's authority. Satan is also portrayed as a twisted serpent which refers to Satan's ability to twist things, calling good *evil* and evil *good.*

Furthermore, God reserves vengeance for Himself (Hebrews 10:30). God, and God alone, is able to punish Satan. A future day is coming when God will destroy Satan, who was created by God. Until then, God allows Satan to exist. God has total dominion over His creation, and He reserves judgment of the heavenly realms to Himself.

As the author Judson Cornwall has said, "It is not our assignment to destroy Satan, for God is not finished with him yet."[1]

Then, God spoke to me from the book of Job:

> Can you draw out Leviathan with a hook, or snare his tongue with a line which you lower? Can you put a reed through his nose, or pierce his jaw with a hook? Will he make many supplications to you? *Will he speak softly to you?* Will he make a covenant with you? Will you take him as a servant forever? Will you play with him as with a bird or will you leash him for your maidens? Will your companions make a banquet of him? Will they apportion him among the merchants? Can you *fill his skin with harpoons,* or his head with fishing spears? Lay your hand on him; *remember the battle—never do it again! Indeed, any hope of overcoming him is false.* No one is so fierce that he would dare stir him up. Who then is able to stand against Me? Who has preceded Me, that I should pay him? Everything under the Heavens is Mine.
>
> —Job 41:1-11, italics mine

God's warning echoed in my spirit: "Who are you to taunt Satan? Who are you to imagine that you can capture Satan? Who are you to make Satan your servant? Or tame Satan as if he were an animal? Or kill Satan by throwing harpoons (or hatchets) at him? To attempt such things is full of presumption, vain imagination, and false hope."

Remember, at one time, even Satan wrongly used authority that God had given him. It led to disobedience, rebellion, and judgment.

THE SOUND OF FURY

When I awoke from the dream, my heart was pounding rapidly. Sitting upright in bed, I kicked off the sheets that were tangled at my feet and swung my legs over the side of the bed. Trying not to wake my wife, I padded to the bathroom and splashed cold water on my face. Slowly, images appeared before me of intercessors who had lost unborn children or had become immobilized by fibromyalgia, leaders who battled depression as well as physical and emotional breakdowns, pastors whose families and churches were ripped apart through schisms, illnesses, and even untimely deaths. Their faces became transposed with the dream's images, and the sounds of their terrifying holocaust echoed through my spirit.

Making my way to the living room, I switched on a light. Unable to sit calmly, I began to pace the floor, interceding for those whose lives had been shattered. It was a chilling nightmare. But with greater clarity, I saw how the enemy had laid a deadly trap for the unsuspecting and well-intentioned within the Body of Christ.

Burying the Hatchet

By the time the sun had risen over the horizon, I had mapped out a plan. When I arrived at my office later that morning, I tracked down phone numbers and began calling various pastors and leaders.

First, I spoke with the pastor who had three pregnant women in his church on the verge of losing their babies. "What is your church doing differently this year?" I asked curiously.

"Nothing, except that we have increased our level of engaging in spiritual warfare," he replied thoughtfully. Venturing further, I asked what kind of warfare. He explained that they were directly coming against and binding demonic principalities of pornography and abortion that hovered over their city.

Sharing the warning dream God had given me the night before, I told him that in wrestling against principalities without sufficient instruction about how to do it and about Satan's counterattacks, he had left himself and his church open to unforeseen and unperceived attack.

"If you stop and repent," I prophesied, "the three women that are now pregnant will go full term in their pregnancies. Their children will live and not die." The day their church repented was the day the three women stopped bleeding. Some months later, all three women gave birth to beautiful, healthy babies.

A similar story emerged from the pastor whose 16-year-old son had run away from home. Throughout the previous year, his church had engaged in spiritual warfare, attempting to bind territorial spirits over their city. As I explained the Scriptures in Job and Isaiah, I felt the presence of God envelop me.

"If God has not directly commanded you to do this kind of spiritual warfare, you are engaged in presumptive behavior. In essence, that is rebellion. Your son is manifesting that rebellion," I prophesied to him. He and his church stopped, and within a week his son came home.

When I called the 42-year-old woman and her daughter who were both pregnant, I learned that recently they had been warring in the heavenly realms. While we discussed aspects of spiritual warfare, I shared with her what God had shown me in my dream and in the Scripture.

I prophesied that if they would stop and repent for presumptive behavior in binding principalities over their city, that both babies would live. Both mother and daughter heeded the warning and repented. God healed them and they continued their pregnancies full term.

Finally, I talked with the pastor whose daughter had chronic fatigue syndrome and fibromyalgia. "I'd like to go over a couple of questions with you," I said. When he agreed, I asked if his daughter had been involved in spiritual warfare that bound high-ranking demonic spirits.

Surprised by the question, he quickly said yes and then added by explanation, "In a vision, my daughter had seen a demonic principality sitting on the dome of the college administration building. She began coming against it." His daughter developed extreme fatigue, depression, and became disoriented within three or four days after attempting to cast down the spirit. As I explained the remedy, I later learned that his daughter did *not* repent of binding the demonic principality over her school. Unfortunately, she remains debilitated by her disease to this day.

THE WISDOM OF RESTRAINT

Over the years, this revelation about spiritual warfare has helped many individuals, families, churches, and leaders. It has become apparent that many of these casualties were not simply a cost of war. Rather, they were unnecessary costs of warfare, fought too often without wisdom.

Like many of you, there have been seasons when I felt invincible, especially when I had ended a fast or a night of prayer. I was armed and dangerous. But I painfully discovered that adopting a *hero* mentality can encourage me to do things that at first seem heroic, but later prove foolish. Without wisdom and restraint, I can easily storm the gates of the enemy in a way that does not accomplish God's purposes and my goals. Instead, it causes me and others near me physical or emotional harm.

Imagine the tragedy of seeing a soldier slaughtered as he jumps out of a foxhole shouting, "You got Johnny. I'll get you." Then as he wildly charges the enemy's machine gun fire, he is cut down in battle. He was fighting a battle that he was destined to lose, because he was outgunned, outmaneuvered, and outwitted. This was not a heroic act.

Likewise, in our zeal to advance the Kingdom of God, we can often lack wisdom in staging spiritual battles. Some battles are necessary, such as when we are attacked and must defend ourselves, or when God commands us to attack demons who have harassed another person. There are already many unavoidable casualties. But to condone and to continue unnecessary losses due to careless spiritual warfare reveals a lack of strategic wisdom. We need to demonstrate greater insight, humility, and restraint as we wage war to subdue the Earth and advance God's Kingdom.

Chapter Three

The Error of Reviling

Every success carries the seeds of its own demise. While there have been remarkable successes attributed to spiritual warfare, much of the fruit, I believe, has come *not* because warfare was done correctly—but due to an increased and unified cry from the Body for prayer and fasting.

Similarly, Mary Baker Eddy, who founded Christian Science, operated with some correct teachings which honored God; her ministry was accompanied by miracles. However, this did not validate her ministry nor her errors. Much of what she taught was the heresy of modern docetic Gnosticism.[2]

Just as miracles did not validate her ministry, neither should some of our seeming successes be allowed to convince us that our attempts in spiritual warfare are wise or even sanctioned by God.

When our actions increase in wisdom and righteousness, God hears our cries and removes principalities and powers governing an area. Then, He showers blessings upon His Church. In times past, had Christians demonstrated similar focus and unified efforts toward intercession, I am convinced that much of the fruit we are seeing today would have appeared even sooner.

In our attempts to engage in spiritual warfare, we need to be prudent and wise. Addressing our prayers about demonic principalities directly to God justifies Him mandating the necessary actions to remove those principalities.

Normally, we are hidden in Christ Jesus (Colossians 3:3), but entering into any level of spiritual warfare exposes us to the sight of the demonic—as if we've stuck our head out of the foxhole. Simply praying to God, asking God to deal with the demonic, is a dimension of spiritual warfare.

THE BATTLE IS THE LORD'S

Asking God to win the battle for us is the wisest way to engage in spiritual warfare, but even that will not prevent demonic counterattack. For example, the apostle Paul recognized that because of his great revelations which were given to destroy the works of the enemy, he was exposed and was given a demonic tormentor to attack him (2 Corinthians 12:7). God allowed the demonic retaliation by the enemy. Thus, we need to learn how to do spiritual warfare wisely (which will be discussed more fully in Chapter Ten).

More than ever, I am convinced that how we handle—or mishandle—spiritual warfare can determine whether or not we expose ourselves and others to injury. Using discernment about spiritual warfare is a major key to avoiding deadly battlegrounds and finding ourselves caught in the enemy's crossfire.

In his book, *The Truth About Angels,* Terry Law writes:

> Without realizing it, many of those who engage in "pulling down" spirits today are really paying tribute to evil angels.[3]

During the early days of the Charismatic movement, many Christians discovered that Satan and his demons were not just a myth, but were real. They tended to embrace an all-or-nothing mentality. Demons were suddenly behind every bush or lurking over everyone's shoulder! Christians began to see most problems as demonic, trying to cast demons out of everyone and everything.

Many overemphasized Satan's power and domain, and thus fell into a similar way of thinking, reminiscent of the Manichaean heresy,[4] which viewed Satan as equal to God and life as only a battle between light and dark forces. However, the Church branded that as heresy. Satan is not God's equal and opposite number. Moreover, life is not simply a battle between light and dark forces. Life is a good heavenly Father rearing sons and daughters for fellowship with Him throughout eternity. There happens to be a war, but it's only a small detail in the grand scheme of history.

When we pay too much attention to evil spirits, we end up paying homage to the strength of the demonic powers rather than to the power of Jesus. While we should engage in many forms of spiritual warfare, we should not be tempted to become so caught up in it that Satan and his hosts subtly become a greater focus than God. Satan would willingly lose every battle to us, so long as he could successfully steal the attention that belongs to God. Whenever we spend more time addressing anything or anyone other than God, our priorities are out of order and Satan receives greater attention. Thereby, he accomplishes his goal.

In his book, *It's God's War*, Judson Cornwall describes how he had fallen into this snare. Standing at the pulpit, he would rebuke the devil so people could worship. Later, the Lord told Judson that He would like to have top billing instead of letting Satan have it. Puzzled, Judson asked God what He meant. God replied by telling Judson that he was exalting demons by recognizing their presence, calling them by name, and telling them what to do.

> It broke my heart to realize that I had unwittingly been leading my congregation into the exaltation of demons. When I asked the Lord what I should do, He sweetly told me to just lead the congregation in praising Him, and He would take care of the demonic activity among us.[5]

These lessons are important for those of us who enter into spiritual warfare. When our belief system is theologically and scripturally sound, and we follow biblical guidance, we can engage in spiritual warfare with minimal danger. However, many

churches today are suffering needless casualties because they have
not followed these guidelines.

Author Leanne Payne, in her book, *Listening Prayer*,
describes her encounters with intercessors who bind demonic
principalities and powers over cities. Furthermore, she calls this
an extreme and dangerous prayer practice.

> Thinking themselves to be intercessors extraordinaire and
> the only ones "doing" spiritual warfare, they were actually
> practicing the presence of demons. They had drawn the
> attention of dark powers toward the Body of Christ in that
> place by praying to them and through pridefully seeing
> themselves as "binding" them. As it turned out, they
> became a channel through which a "principality and
> power"—a ruling spirit over that city—descended into our
> midst…
>
> Needless to say, we were brought into a spiritual
> conflict of unusual proportions, one that need never [have]
> occurred. These folk, thinking they were intercessors, had
> merely succeeded in informing the powers of darkness in,
> over, and around that city that we were coming! In
> listening to them proudly relate all their hair-raising tussles
> with dark powers, I realized they take this "gift" every place
> they go. The way they pray assures that the people they are
> involved with will have dramatic and terrible
> confrontations with evil powers, and that some of them
> will come under serious demonic deception. This is
> dangerous error.[6]

Leanne Payne believes those who bind demonic principalities in the heavenly realms are straying from the scriptural model of Jesus. She writes that Jesus focused on God the Father, and thus taught us to pray to God rather than addressing demonic powers in the heavenly realms. She encourages readers to fix their eyes on Jesus and talk to Him. It is Jesus who will deliver His people from the snares of the evil one. We must remember that the battle is the Lord's, as King David said when he slew Goliath (1 Samuel 17:47).

Nothing New Under the Sun

Recently, spiritual warfare teachings have embraced the concept of taking authority and binding spirits over geographic areas around the world. We might tend to think this is a new weapon used against the enemy. However, such teaching has been around since the early Church.

> That which has been is what will be, that which is done is what will be done, and there is nothing new under the sun.
> –Ecclesiastes 1:9

> That which is has already been, and what is to be has already been; and God requires an account of what is past.
> –Ecclesiastes 3:15

A wise heart knows the proper time and procedure. For
there is a proper time and procedure for every delight,
when a man's trouble is heavy upon him.
                                    –Ecclesiastes 8:5b-6, NASB

The apostle Peter and Jude warned the early Church not to
engage in spiritual warfare wrongly, especially by reviling Satan.

And the angels who did not keep their proper domain, but
left their own abode, He has reserved in everlasting chains
under darkness for the judgment on the great
day...Likewise also these dreamers defile the flesh, reject
authority, and speak evil of dignitaries. Yet Michael the
archangel, in contending with the devil, when he disputed
about the body of Moses, *dared not* bring a reviling
accusation against him, but said, "The Lord rebuke you!"
                                    –Jude 6-9, italics mine

SPEAKING DISDAINFULLY

In our attempts at spiritual warfare, are we guilty of reviling
celestial beings? By definition, *reviling* involves verbal abuse,
railing, or scolding—quarreling noisily, rebuking angrily.[7]

In this passage above, Jude was stating that if we make
disparaging remarks and harshly accuse spiritual beings—good or
evil—we will have departed from Jesus' courteous ways and have
become like the enemy against whom we wrestle.

Courtesy is the hallmark of God's Kingdom. Discourtesy is the trademark of Satan's. When contending with the devil, Jesus spoke firmly but with the utmost respect. He did not revile when answering Satan's temptations. Nor did Jesus speak rudely, disrespectfully, or call Satan demeaning names. Rather, Jesus simply quoted Scripture to rebuke the devil.

As a former high ranking angel of great eminence and power, Satan is *not* to be treated with dishonor. God created Satan with a keen intellect and incredible authority, and He gave him a position near the throne (Ezekiel 28). Although Satan became evil and God removed his authority through our risen Lord Jesus, He did not remove Satan's gifts. All gifts from God are irrevocable (Romans 11:29). For example, many rock groups today are formed by former church members who sung in the choir and led worship. Though they have fallen in their relationship with God, He has not removed their gift of music that was originally intended for worship.

Recognizing Satan's created giftedness, the archangel Michael, who also possessed high rank and authority, fought only in compliance with God's courteous nature. If Michael did not presume to revile Satan, doesn't it seem foolish for us to do so?

FALSE SENSE OF POWER

Many Christians have entered into deliverance ministry or spiritual warfare assuming that reviling Satan somehow assures them of more power. However, doing so actually defeats all of us.

Whenever we hurl insulting abuse or vent our anger at the enemy, we violate God's created order and invite destructive counterattacks.

When Satan fell, he took with him heavenly beings (Revelation 12:9). Therefore, it stands to reason that many who fell with Satan would also have held high rank. For example, most of Satan's followers who rebelled were probably those angels nearest to him and under his authority. Most likely, they were his peers or those lesser in rank. And just like Satan, they probably fell from their lofty positions due to the same sin of pride (Isaiah 14:11-14; 1 Timothy 3:6). When these celestial dignitaries fell into the second Heaven, Satan would naturally have assigned them to positions of authority comparable to that which they had previously held in the third Heaven.[8] They would also therefore have retained the giftings commensurate to their positions. God would not have repealed their gifts and violated His law. He only revoked their right to commingle in the third Heaven.

We need to be careful if we think the Holy Spirit has called us to address such mighty spiritual beings. As His followers, we must retain the nature of Jesus in *all* that we do. Moreover, we must be aware of the possibility and likelihood that these demonic beings possess gifts that may far outsmart and outmaneuver us.

A FUTURE PROMISE

Although Scripture says that Jesus raised us up and made us sit together in the heavenly places in Christ Jesus (Ephesians 2:6), the fullness of our heavenly position will be manifest in the ages to come. At present, we are not seated in fullness in the heavenly places. But in the ages to come, we have a promise that we will sit with God and at that time, we will judge angels. Until then, we have been made a little lower than the angels (Hebrews 2:6-7). Consequently, we should not command the angels or any other celestial dignitary. Otherwise we are exercising a pseudo-authority, thus drawing unnecessary demonic counterattack which we are ill-equipped to withstand.

GOD WILL DELIVER US

Another warning about cursing or reviling high-ranking principalities and powers in the second Heaven is found in the second epistle of Peter:

> *The Lord knows how to deliver* the godly out of temptations and to reserve the unjust under punishment for the day of judgment....They are not afraid to *speak evil of dignitaries*, whereas angels, who are greater in power and might, *do not bring a reviling accusation against them* before the Lord.
>
> —2 Peter 2:9-11, italics mine

Satan has fallen from his originally created position as the anointed cherub of God who had great authority and responsibility to protect and defend the holy mountain of God

(Ezekiel 28:14). He is a defeated foe, yet he still retains the
dignity of his former position until eternity is inaugurated. Then,
God will bind and cast him into the lake of fire. In the meantime,
even God's archangels respond cautiously to Satan. ·

Further evidence of this is found in the book of Zechariah.
Here, even Joshua the high priest and the Angel of the Lord knew
their inadequacy in fighting with Satan.

> Then he showed me Joshua the high priest standing before
> the Angel of the Lord, and Satan standing at his right hand
> to oppose him. And the Lord said to Satan, "*The Lord
> rebuke you, Satan!* The Lord who has chosen Jerusalem
> rebuke you! Is this not a brand plucked from the fire?"
> Now Joshua was clothed with filthy garments and was
> standing before the Angel. Then He answered and spoke to
> those who stood before Him, saying, "Take away the filthy
> garments from him." And to him He said, "See I have
> removed your iniquity from you and I will clothe you with
> rich robes."
>
> –Zechariah 3:1-4, italics mine

Seeing Satan as a powerful, evil ruler and treating him with
respect by not reviling him or his demonic forces is essential.
Through this kind of respect, we leave intact God's divine
protocol (correct procedure). We can call on the Lord to rebuke
Satan. But to do more, to rail against Satan, carries a harsh
penalty—needless suffering, destruction, or untimely death.

As I have mentioned, you do not defeat the devil by becoming like him. Nor do you defeat him by speaking accusingly or angrily at him. Since this is an important point, please allow me restate it: the hallmark of God's Kingdom is *courtesy* and respect; the hallmark of Satan's kingdom is rudeness, brazenness, and impertinence.

Ignorance is not bliss; it comes with a stiff penalty. Ignorance can open spiritual doors through which Satan has an opportunity to attack us. We are warned that we are destroyed for lack of knowledge. Sometimes partial knowledge can prove deadly.

THE DANGER OF PRIDE

When we assault spirits of abortion, pornography, false religions or even religiousness over a city or geographic region, we can be tempted to battle in our own strength and understanding. Remember what God told Zerubbabel:

"Not by *might* nor by power, but by My Spirit," says the Lord of hosts.

–Zechariah 4:6b, italics mine

While it sounds impressive to discern the names of demonic principalities, such a practice can easily mislead us into demonstrating pride in our spiritual prowess.

Often we are led to believe that the Gospel can now go forth in a city because we have bound principalities in the high places. But, what if there were other factors that played into this spiritual equation and displayed seeming victory? Such factors can serve as a decoy maneuver by the enemy to make us think that we are winning, and thus lure us deeper into his trap.

Our pride from an apparent victory can be blinding. When victories begin to happen, we can become puffed up about our own abilities. In fact, Scripture says that knowledge can puff up (1 Corinthians 8:1).

This is all part of Satan's tactics. In fact, one of the ways Satan counterattacks is to cause us to be proud that we are "mighty warriors for God." Our inward, quiet boasting opens the door for him to defile and eventually frustrate everything we may have begun. By this practice, we may give him access to us and those around us, and thus, we become needless casualties of war.

When we begin to pridefully strategize, we can easily fall into the heresy of Gnosticism, a term derived from the Greek work *gnosis* which means knowledge.[9] Gnosticism is the subtle and dangerous teaching that we are saved through knowledge.

While it may be beneficial to develop spiritual strategies, an overemphasis may leave us thinking that we can ascend to the Heavens through the acquisition of knowledge.

In spiritual mapping, warriors track out the history and localities of demonic activity in buildings, cities, regions, states, or nations. This informs them how and where to focus prayers of repentance and deliverance. In spiritual warfare, and in many other fields, to do research is good—and often necessary. Information gleaned from spiritual mapping and books like John Dawson's *Taking Our Cities for God* may be incredibly resourceful in helping us form strong prayers of identification repentance. These are powerful tools that God endorses. But mere knowledge is only part of the strategy.

When we engage in spiritual warfare, we can become endangered by our own knowledge and by the enemy, if we do not learn to take our stand in the cross and die to pride that can arise from our knowledge. Operating in knowledge, like operating in the flesh, may be perilous when we face a powerful foe. As in all things, it may be easy to get caught up in knowledge and strategies of spiritual warfare. But as intercessors, we must ask ourselves where to draw the line.

To operate in our own understanding is exceedingly dangerous in spiritual warfare. In so doing, we may be operating in our own soul power. Hence, we would be doomed to tragedy and suffering and to operating within the limits of mere humanity. During such times, we may get a false sense of unlimited presence, power, and knowledge when in reality this dunamis of God has begun to escape our grasp, much like trying to pick up a handful of sand.

BLAME SHIFTING

As intercessors we can unknowingly shift the blame for our cities' problems to Satan, rather than taking responsibility for the darkness we have caused in our land. In doing so, we imitate our forefather, Adam, who blamed God and Eve for causing him to sin.

The woman whom You gave to be with me, she gave me of the tree, and I ate.

–Genesis 3:12

Blaming only causes us to deny our responsibility and to point our fingers at someone or something other than ourselves. In essence, this describes a victim mentality. But the painful truth is that *we* are the real problem. We have a heart that is evil and often chooses sin over righteousness!

> For out of the heart proceed evil thoughts, murders, adulteries, fornications, thefts, false witness, blasphemies.
>
> –Matthew 15:19

We are our own worst enemy. Satan is not the first or major problem. God took care of Satan two millennia ago, when Jesus defeated him and regained authority in the Earth. God has promised us the victory.

> But thanks be to God, who gives us the victory through our Lord Jesus Christ.
>
> –1 Corinthians 15:57

We need not vent our anger, shake our fist, stomp our feet, and revile Satan. The Bible encourages us to humble ourselves, repent and ask God to remove principalities that curse our land.

When we are *not* humble and repentant, we are incapable of removing demonic principalities by our commands. Only God has the authority to assign or extricate principalities in the Heavens. And He chooses to do so according to our responses.

When we change our hearts and our actions, God hears from Heaven and heals our land (2 Chronicles 7:14). Since the beginning of time, mankind has never healed the land except through expressing repentance.

FROM THE HIGH PLACES OF INDIA

In 1998, while I was in Bombay, India, ministering at a leaders' conference, I met a sullen and despondent pastor and his wife. At one time, the young couple had high hopes for church growth and regional impact, and were full of great expectations. Then they became heavily involved in spiritual warfare.

Living on a hill in Southern India that overlooked the surrounding countryside, which was punctuated by ancient Hindu temples, they began to try to conquer the high places in the spirit world. Attempting to contend with spirits of poverty, death, and reincarnation among others, they demanded that Satan loose his grip over the Indian people.

Shortly after they began to assault the powers of darkness, an elderly neighbor died. Although the wizened old woman had professed Christianity, she still persisted in clinging to a mixture of various Hindu rituals.

One morning, as the pastor passed her house, he smelled the rot of human flesh that filled the hot, musty tropical air. Soon, he discovered the neighbor's badly decomposed body lying in the undergrowth near her house.

That night, the pastor's wife saw an apparition—an evil spirit that resembled their dead neighbor—enter their bedroom. The ghost flung a black scarf across the bedroom that floated through the air like a leaf and landed on the couple's bed.

The next day, the young pastor had a heart attack and nearly died. For two weeks, he hovered between life and death, and he suffered two more heart attacks. His wife also became deathly ill. Delirious with fever, she was hospitalized with a serious intestinal disorder.

After they were released from the hospital, a gardener who worked at their home told them with scorn and ridicule: "Nothing is going to live here. You are outside of your authority. You are taking on something greater and more powerful than yourselves."

With growing fear and dread, the young couple watched everything around them die—their beloved pets, livestock, plants, flowers, and fruit trees. Almost overnight the atmosphere surrounding their home became eerie and ominous—highly charged with demonic activity.

One morning as they were leaving their property they were shaken to see that the rod-iron spears lining their gate had buckled and now resembled cobra heads bent over and prepared to attack.

When I met them six months after they began warring in the Heavens, they looked lifeless. I encouraged them to stop this type of warfare. Through prayer, I discerned that the calamities were able to take root in their lives because they had lost spiritual authority by misunderstanding and violating God's principles that govern the spiritual universe. I exhorted them to ask God's forgiveness for disputing His authority structure in the Heavens.

I also asked them to bring a white cloth to the evening service to counteract the vision of the black scarf. That night, pastors from around India laid hands on the cloth and anointed it with oil. The Holy Spirit prompted me to instruct the pastor's wife to stand in her bedroom, exactly where the apparition stood, and in the same manner toss the cloth on the bed saying, "I rebuke every evil thing that has come upon this house from a result of the curse of this woman. We repent of violating God's created order through errant spiritual warfare."

After the pastor and his wife repented and reversed the curse, their health improved. Furthermore, the doctor pronounced the pastor's heart to be as good as new. No scar tissue was found on his heart muscle.

A month later, I received word that everything around their house had begun to live again. Plants, chickens, dogs, and cats thrived. Even more surprising, the following morning after they reversed the curse, the cobra shaped rod-iron spears on their gate miraculously straightened! And the gardener disappeared.

Chapter Four

Parameters of Authority

RIGHTLY ENGAGING in spiritual warfare boils down to a simple issue of authority. Authority, or the Greek word *exousia*, refers to the right to use power, to take action, to issue commands, and to respond in obedience.

Before we can operate with authority, we need to first understand whose authority it is, under whom we operate. Second, we need to recognize and submit to authority over us. Third, we need to know the parameters of authority. Fourth, we need to determine the rules of engagement (how to fight) so that our authority will not be lost.

Having God's authority and using His power is wonderful. But, authority is easy to misuse. Some years ago when John Sandford was visiting a friend in Boston, the Lord opened his eyes. He saw the trees weeping. When he asked his friend why, she said that when hurricanes had traveled along the coastline to New England threatening havoc and destruction, they had prayed with presumption.

"We didn't ask God if we should pray," she confessed. "We just took our authority and commanded the hurricanes not to come inland. They didn't. But we didn't realize that the hurricanes brought the needed rains. We've had a drought for seven years."

LINES OF AUTHORITY

In the same way, we have been entrusted with incredible authority. But we must use our authority correctly. We must not presume in advance what to do and then consult God, expecting Him to bless our actions. We need to guard against impatience and not force God to act.

Jesus showed us the proper way to use authority. He did nothing on His own authority, but only what the Father told Him to do.

> ...the Son can do nothing of Himself, but what He sees the Father do; for whatever He does, the Son also does *in like manner.*
>
> –John 5:19, italics mine

ON THE FIRING LINE

In the movie, *Navy Seals*, there was a young naval officer who was ordered by his commanding officer to carry out a stealth infiltration/exfiltration operation. Although the officer was gifted, he constantly endangered missions by taking unnecessary gambles. On one mission, everything was going like clockwork until the young officer ran out from cover and fired on the enemy, although he had prior orders *not* to do so. Consequently, he endangered the mission and the people around him. As a result, a team member died in a deadly firefight.

A similar loss of judgment is illustrated in the movie, *Saving Private Ryan.* Tom Hanks plays a Ranger infantry captain who is ordered to find Private Ryan and escort him to safety. In one scene, Hanks' character has a tragic loss of judgment. His judgment is clouded not because of thrill-seeking or ego gratification, but because of battle fatigue. He orders his unit into an unnecessary skirmish that has little to do with his mission. They succeed, but at a great cost—they lose valuable team members.

Likewise, we can disjoint a spiritual warfare maneuver. Whenever we act on our own thought processes in isolation from the Body of Christ, the enemy comes sweeping through the flank we've left open.

A good soldier learns when to go for battlefield opportunities and when to let them pass. Underlying this teaching is a very simple concept and one that new recruits at the Ranger School in Fort Benning, Georgia, have drilled into them during training:

It's not your job to be a hero on the battlefield. Instead, your first order of business is to survive. Your second order of business is the continued survival of both yourself and those with you. Your third order of business, then, is to achieve your commander's intent, or to secure the mission.[10]

As General Patton said to his troops in 1945 when he commanded the Third Army: "No one ever won a war by dying for his country. He won it by making the other guy give *his* life for his country."[11]

DELEGATED AUTHORITY

To gain a fuller understanding of authority, we can look at the book of Genesis when man was first given authority. In the beginning, God gave Adam and Eve authority to subdue everything that moved on the face of the Earth. Adam had a mandate to subdue the land.

God commissioned Adam to name the animals. That was significant, because to name an animal meant assigning to the animal its character, purpose, and destiny. In other words, naming something signified what that created being was destined to live out and become. God's principle is the same, whether it's naming animals or humans.

Furthermore, naming something gives authority over it. For example, God named Adam, because He had authority over Adam. Adam named the animals because he was given authority over the creatures. Adam named Eve because he was given authority over her. And as his wife, Eve shared Adam's authority. This is still true today. Parents name their children, because they have authority over them.

Adam had dominion over the Earth—sky, land, and sea. When God told Adam to tend the garden and to subdue the Earth, He turned over to Adam everything on the Earth. In other words, God established lines of authority in the Earth through the same authority structure He gave to Adam. This is the basis of our authority in spiritual warfare.

When Adam was hungry, he could simply command the Earth to produce food. And it did. Adam and Eve did not know hunger, sickness, or death. Their Garden of Eden was a paradise beyond imagination from which they were to subdue the Earth. However, they failed.

The serpent, who also had been named by Adam, planned to establish his dominion over all of creation—thereby attempting to exalt himself higher than God (Isaiah 14:13-14). The serpent's goal wasn't simply to attack Adam or Eve. They merely possessed what he really wanted—authority over the Earth.

Crafting a cunning deception, the serpent twisted God's words, suggesting that Adam and Eve eat fruit from a tree God had prohibited. If they ate from it, Satan said they would become like God. However, when Adam ate the fruit, he did not become like God. Instead, his God-given authority to subdue the Earth was ripped away, usurped by the deceptive serpent.

Through disobedience, Adam succumbed to Satan's plans. By placing Satan's word above God's Word, Adam was now an underling in Satan's kingdom. Furthermore, Adam had now subjected the Earth to satanic corruption.

A World in Chaos

For thousands of years, the serpent had authority over the Earth. He used his authority to destroy God's work. Everything the serpent touched began to die and disintegrate. Man began to die spiritually in sin, and therefore, everything on the Earth became impregnated with and suffered from that sin. The Earth began to deteriorate.

The Earth is also defiled under its inhabitants, because they have transgressed the laws, changed the ordinance, broken the everlasting covenant. Therefore *the curse has devoured the Earth*, and those who dwell in it are desolate.
                                          –Isaiah 24:5-6a, italics mine

For the earnest expectation of the creation eagerly waits for the revealing of the sons of God. For the *creation was subjected to futility, not willingly*, but because of Him who subjected it in hope.
                                          –Romans 8:19-20, italics mine

Eventually, everything man touched became infected with the same stain that threatened to bring chaos out of God's created order. The Earth began to depart from God's creative order. Continents began to drift apart.

To Eber were born two sons...one was Peleg, for in his days *the Earth was divided...*
                                          –Genesis 10:25, italics mine

Geological plates below the Earth began sliding against each other and earthquakes shook the land. Magma began to erupt. Volcanoes were born. Plagues and pestilence were released across the Earth. In every way and in many forms, the Earth began to war against itself.

A domino effect began to take place in creation, the solar system, and far-reaching galaxies. The creative order began spinning out of order. Chaos ensued. All of creation began to groan: *Put an end to this misery. Put an end to the chaos on Earth* (Romans 8:19-21).

In the fullness of time, the One who created the Heavens and the Earth, Jesus Christ, left His heavenly throne and entered into His creation.

When Jesus began His earthly ministry to destroy the works of the devil, He fasted 40 days (Luke 4:2). At the end of that time, Satan, who had taken authority over the Earth from Adam, offered it back to Jesus for a price—Jesus must bow down and worship Satan.

> And the devil said to Him, "All this authority I will give You, and their glory; for this has been delivered to me, and I give it to whomever I wish. Therefore if You will worship before me, all will be Yours." And Jesus answered and said to him, "Get behind Me, Satan! For it is written, 'You shall worship the Lord your God, and Him only you shall serve.'"
>
> –Luke 4:6-8

When Jesus quoted Luke 4:8 to Satan, it became poignant with even deeper meaning because Jesus was actually saying, "*You* (Satan) shall worship the Lord *your* God and Him only shall *you* serve." Jesus was reminding Satan that although he had authority on Earth, God had authority over Satan. Jesus was also serving notice that He had come to legally take Satan's ill-gotten authority away from him. Moreover, Jesus was reminding Satan that though he had temporary authority over the Earth, God had supreme authority over Satan as well as the entire cosmos.

Last year in England, when I was speaking on this particular passage, an unusual phenomenon happened. Using several microphone stands to illustrate my teaching, I had placed a purple cloth on one stand to represent the authority God had given to Adam. On another, I had placed a black cloth to represent the serpent.

To demonstrate Satan seizing authority from Adam, I draped the purple cloth on top of the black one. Then I related the story of Jesus being tempted by Satan. To dramatize what Jesus said, I pointed at the microphone stand and said, "You, Satan, shall worship the Lord *your* God and Him only shall *you* serve." Suddenly the microphone stand began to bow without anyone touching it. More than 3,000 people in the room gasped, then cheered and shouted as the stand, representing Satan, cowered to the floor.

AUTHORITY REVOKED FROM SATAN

After His death, Jesus descended into hell (1 Peter 3:19). There, Jesus stripped all authority from Satan. Authority to rule the Earth was returned to Jesus. We know that happened because of what

Jesus said to His disciples just before He ascended to the Father:

> And Jesus came and spoke to them, saying, "All authority
> has been given to Me *in Heaven and on Earth*."
> —Matthew 28:18, italics mine

In other words, Jesus has legal authority in the Heavens and on the Earth. He had never lost authority in the Heavens, but Jesus regained authority on the Earth. When Adam sinned, nothing changed in the heavenly realms. God's rule and reign had never been threatened. However, Jesus prevailed as the Lion of the tribe of Judah, the Root of David (Revelation 5:5) and restored to mankind the authority to subdue the Earth.

When Adam sinned in the Garden of Eden, authority that God had given mankind was handed over to Satan. As Ezekiel 18:4 says, "the soul who sins shall die." The law of sowing and reaping requires death for sin. By laying down His life willingly— through His crucifixion, burial, and resurrection—Jesus, the Creator who came as a man, could now legally claim what had been taken from mankind.

Adam's sin of disobedience resulted in death, but Jesus' act of obedience resulted in life. That's why the apostle Paul called Jesus the *last Adam*. Jesus did what the first Adam failed to do—retain the authority to subdue the Earth (Romans 5:14-15; 1 Corinthians 15:45-49).

Jesus returned the original mandate to the Church to subdue the Earth—not the Heavens—and to have dominion over everything that moves on the face of the Earth, including demonic forces that would infringe upon the Kingdom of God and our subduing the Earth. Jesus has delegated to us limited Kingdom authority until eternity is inaugurated. Then, we will rule and reign in the Heavens with Him.

Although mankind abdicated authority to the enemy, God gave mankind a second chance—He always does, because He is full of love, mercy, and forgiveness. God has always believed in us to fulfill His created purpose. His love bears for us whatever we cannot bear. His love believes in us when we have lost ability to believe in ourselves. His love hopes for us when we have lost hope. His love endures everything we do (1 Corinthians 13:7.)

WHY DO WE STILL HAVE PROBLEMS

If we have been given authority to subdue the Earth, why do we still have problems? First, because Satan wants man's authority back. He wasn't afraid to rebel against God in the beginning. Do you think he's afraid now? Absolutely not. Satan has power today because God gave him power. God does not remove the gifts He gives, which verifies His integrity to His written Word (Romans 11:29). Satan, though fallen, still has the original gifts given to him by God at his creation.

Second, though God has given the Earth back to us to subdue, we have not yet accomplished it. We have been commissioned to subdue it like leaven in a barrel of meal (Matthew 13:33). The Kingdom of God is to *leaven* the whole Earth. The first fruit of that destruction of darkness—

and the spreading of light—was provided at Calvary.

So, Satan has power, but he does not have authority to stop what God has commanded the Church to do. Satan does retain the power of deception and seduction to cause us to think that he has authority, but he does not. We are called to exercise our God-given power and authority to destroy the works of the evil one in our proper earthly sphere of authority.

To understand our authority and how it operates, we need to understand how far our authority extends and the limitations God has placed on our jurisdiction.

Let's look at two heavenly realms which includes the second and third Heavens. We will also look at an earthly realm, which I refer to as terrestrial. As believers who are entrusted with the task of advancing the Kingdom of God on the Earth, I believe that God has given authority to operate in only *one* of these realms.

Chapter Five

Warfare in the Second Heaven

I N THE VAST EXPANSE of the universe, a multiplicity of heavenly realms co-exist above our earthly realm. The third Heaven, or the "Heaven of Heavens" according to Nehemiah 9:6, is the dwelling place of God's throne and all benevolent spiritual beings such as archangels and angels, as well as the seraphim and the cheribum who surround God's throne and protect His radiant glory.

Another heavenly realm, which I refer to as the second Heaven, is the command post of Satan and his diabolical spiritual dignitaries which include principalities, powers, rulers of darkness, and spiritual hosts of wickedness.

According to Scripture, Jesus Christ created thrones, dominions, principalities, and powers. Seated far above them, Jesus has dominion over all of them.

For *by Him all things were created* that are in Heaven and
that are on Earth, visible and invisible, whether thrones or
dominions or *principalities or powers.* All things were
created through Him and for Him.

—Colossians 1:16, italics mine

Which He worked in Christ Jesus when He raised Him
from the dead and seated Him at His right hand in the
heavenly places, *far above all principality and power* and
might and dominion, and every name that is named, not
only in this age but also in that which is to come.

—Ephesians 1:20-21, italics mine

Who has gone into Heaven and is at the right hand of
God, *angels and authorities and powers having been made
subject to Him.*

—1 Peter 3:22, italics mine

A HEAVENLY ARMY

God created countless numbers of spirit beings who are normally
invisible to us, unless God opens our eyes—which He did for
Elisha and his servant when the armies of Syria surrounded his
house (2 Kings 6:17).

Angels, which is translated as *messengers* in the Greek and
Hebrew, are commissioned to bring messages from God, to
minister to people, or to administer the judgments of God.

Angels may relay specific instructions from God and have specific tasks to fulfill such as healing, strengthening, or encouraging us.

> For He shall give His angels charge over you, to keep you in all your ways. In their hands they shall bear you up, lest you dash your foot against a stone.
> —Psalm 91:11-12

> Are they not all ministering spirits sent forth to minister for those who will inherit salvation?
> —Hebrews 1:14

> The Angel of the Lord encamps all around those who fear Him, and delivers them.
> —Psalm 34:7

Angels have bodies of light that can be seen or felt. They are mighty, powerful, intelligent, and glorious supernatural beings. For example, an angel freed Peter from prison (Acts 12:5-11). Another angel killed 185,000 Assyrians (2 Kings 19:35). Still another rolled back the huge stone from the doorway of Jesus' tomb (Matthew 28:2).

The third Heaven has a highly developed ranking structure. Angels and other heavenly beings have various functions, positions, and distinctions. Some angels minister to humans on the Earth, while others stand in the immediate presence of God (Luke 1:19). Regardless of their eminent ranking, the entire angelic hierarchy operates on God's authority structure. All are submissive to the sovereign will of God.

Among the celestial hierarchy are three mighty and powerful
leaders: Michael who is identified as *the* archangel and is one
of the chief princes (Daniel 10:13), Gabriel who stands in the
presence of God and is a special messenger of God, and Satan
who was once an anointed cherub who walked in the midst of
God's fiery stones, but who rebelled and now directs a host of
dark angels.

Many scholars believe that Isaiah 14 paints a verbal picture
of Satan:

> How you are fallen from Heaven, O Lucifer, son of the
> morning! How you are cut down to the ground, you who
> weakened the nations! For you have said in your heart: 'I
> will ascend into Heaven, I will exalt my throne above the
> stars of God; I will also sit on the mount of the
> congregation on the farthest sides of the north; I will
> ascend above the heights of the clouds, I will be like the
> Most High.'
>
> –Isaiah 14:12-14

Because he led a rebellion, Satan and his followers were hurled
out of the third Heaven into the second Heaven and to Earth.

> And war broke out in Heaven: Michael and his angels
> fought against the dragon; and the dragon and his angels
> fought, but they did not prevail, nor was a place found for
> them in Heaven any longer. So the great dragon was cast
> out, that serpent of old, called the Devil and Satan, who

deceives the whole world; *he was cast to the Earth, and his*
angels were cast out with him.

                                                   –Revelation 12:7-9, italics mine

Although he has limited liberty on the Earth, Satan reigns over
his demonic kingdom. Scripture describes Satan as the god of this
world who blinds people's minds to God's truth (2 Corinthians 4:4).

From the second Heaven, Satan orchestrates rebellion and
anarchy around the world. His personal, primary mission is to
hinder the work of God and to gain control of the Earth again.

Hence, the name Satan means *adversary*.[12] Satan's activity is
always directed against God and His people. A primary way Satan
opposes God is by counterfeiting God's authority. He is the
master of deception.

Satan's method is always to distract and ensnare. He wants to
lure our attention away from God. He promotes false worship
and produces counterfeit supernatural wonders. He prowls
around seeking to devour men and women (1 Peter 5:8).

Satan tries to tempt believers with evil desires and to weaken
the Church. Through his demonic forces, he plants doubts,
spreads accusations, and promotes divisions in the Body of
Christ. He oppresses Christians and causes incurable sickness,
diseases, and all manner of injustices.

Satan cunningly devises schemes of rebellion and seeks to
advance darkness through moral corruption, sexual perversion,
and every other evil behavior. He deceives nations, influences
world governments, world economies, international politics,
global entertainment, education, the media, and even religion.

He also works through social systems that oppress the poor and the weak.

Since Satan counterfeits whatever God creates, Satan appointed principalities in the second Heaven to rule and acquire dominion over nations. These second Heaven principalities have great power, presence, and importance by means of the rank which was theirs before they fell.

Having been principalities in the third Heaven, and now only in the second, they still retain positional distinction despite their loss of grace and dignity. Furthermore, these second Heaven principalities gain dominion by continuing treachery, lawlessness, violence, pride, and deception on the Earth.

Chapter Six

Terrestrial Warfare

W HEN GOD SEPARATED the Heavens and the Earth, He made the arch of the sky and divided the waters. Dry land appeared and the seas were formed. He called forth plants, trees, and vegetation of every kind. He established the seasons. Everything that moved on the face of the Earth—birds, animals and sea creatures—were formed. Then, God made man in His image.

Everything within this life-sustaining biosphere, which the Bible calls terrestrial (1 Corinthians 15:40), was placed under man's domain. Every creature on the face of the Earth, atmospheric conditions surrounding the globe, as well as demonic spirits operating in this earthly realm were included in the arena of man's rule.

While high-ranking demons operate in the second Heaven, lower-ranking demons infiltrate our terrestrial habitat. They are ruled by the high-ranking principalities in the second Heaven which are what the apostle Paul lists as rulers, powers, world forces of darkness, and spiritual forces of wickedness in the heavenly places (Ephesians 6:12).

Lower-ranking demons in the terrestrial realm function as infantry in Satan's kingdom. These terrestrial demons are disembodied spirits that are capable of entering into or coming out of humans (Matthew 12:43-45). The better they are at hiding their presence, the stronger and more entrenched they become. Their goal is to remain within a person until the person's influence is overcome, the person has fulfilled demonically inspired tasks of wounding and destroying others, or the person is dead.

In the book, *A Comprehensive Guide to Deliverance and Inner Healing*, John and Mark Sandford have written:

> Demons seek to enter people for many reasons, probably foremost because they seek to destroy God's temple. But another reason is that it is a delight to be encased in flesh. Remember that Jesus said that when a demon goes out of a man, it wanders about "seeking rest" (Matthew 12:43).[13]

Like marauders, demons may come and go or take up permanent residence in people, buildings, and objects, but they seem to prefer dwelling in human hosts.

Author Gary Kinnaman noted in his book, *Angels Dark and Light*:

...It seems that they (demons) are able to influence a single person, object, place often for long periods of time... Demons then, may be found haunting buildings or other specific locales; associating themselves with material objects or possessing animals; oppressing families, perhaps for generations; possessing people by entering their bodies, something commonly called "demonization;" or exercising hellish influence over nations, regions, geographical territories, and cities.[14]

Seeking to invade and conquer, demons have miraculous powers and are always seeking to deceive mankind by false guidance and false prophecy. Their objective is to distract and hinder humans. Therefore, they lie, cause discord and division, entice, deceive, enslave, torment, drive, and compel men and women toward evil. They can also cause blindness, insanity, suicidal thoughts, physical defects and deformities, and other illnesses.

God permits Satan and his demonic hosts to continue doing evil in the Earth for several reasons:

1. To maintain humility in our lives (2 Corinthians 12:7).
2. To develop faith and righteousness in our lives (James 1:12; 1 Peter 1:7-13; 5:8-9; 2 Peter 1:4-9; Jude 20-24).
3. To bring about trials whereby we can be rewarded when we overcome (1 John 2:13; 4:1-6; Revelation 2:7, 11, 17, 26-28; 3:5, 12, 21).
4. To teach us how to fight (Judges 3:2).
5. To afflict us in order that we may repent (Job 33:14-30; 1 Corinthians 5:1-6).

6. To demonstrate the power of God over satanic power (Mark 1:21-27; 16:17-20; Acts 13:6-10; Ephesians 3:10).

For the present, two powerful forces operate in this terrestrial arena—the power of God and the power of Satan. Throughout the Bible, there are repeated references of a contest between God's Kingdom and Satan's kingdom:

> But the Prince of the kingdom of Persia withstood me twenty-one days; and behold, Michael, one of the chief Princes, came to help me. For I had been left alone there with the kings of Persia.
>
> —Daniel 10:13

> Let the high praises of God be in their mouth, and a two-edged sword in their hand; to execute vengeance on the nations and punishments on the peoples; to bind their kings with chains, and their nobles with fetters of iron; to execute on them the written judgement...
>
> —Psalm 149:6-9

THE INCARNATION OF JESUS

When Jesus left His heavenly realm and took the form of flesh, Heaven's power was manifested on the Earth to destroy Satan's works. Jesus could have accomplished it from His throne in

Heaven simply by commanding it to be so. But, instead Jesus entered into our terrestrial arena to return authority to mankind.

> ...For this purpose the Son of God was manifested, that He might destroy the works of the devil.
>
> –1 John 3:8

At the beginning of His ministry, Jesus announced His purpose in coming to the Earth:

> The Spirit of the Lord is upon Me, because He has anointed Me to preach the gospel to the poor; He has sent Me to heal the brokenhearted, to proclaim liberty to the captives and recovery of sight to the blind, to set at liberty those who are oppressed; to proclaim the acceptable year of the Lord.
>
> –Luke 4:18-19

Jesus healed the sick, cleansed the lepers, raised the dead, and delivered people from demons. In so doing, He modeled terrestrial spiritual warfare.

How Jesus dealt with demons and thus accomplished spiritual warfare is the most original and striking feature of His entire ministry. Jews living in Israel during the time of Jesus had recognized the reality of demons and already practiced some forms of exorcism. But the measure of authority with which Jesus cast out demons had never been seen. It was astounding. It came forcefully and with true dramatic results. Jesus described it as a clash of two spiritual kingdoms.

When Jesus cast out demons, there were powerful physical manifestations. Demons threw people to the ground before Him crying out and proclaiming His heavenly authority (Mark 3:11). Some caused convulsions in humans before they would leave (Mark 9:20, 26).

Most whom Jesus delivered were religious Jews. They weren't heathens who practiced witchcraft or idolatry. Nor were they criminals or people branded as insane. They were simply God's people whom the evil one had harassed and tormented.

People marveled at Jesus' authority over demons:

> Then *they were all amazed*, so that they questioned among themselves…For with authority He commands even the unclean spirits and they obey Him…And He was preaching in their synagogues throughout all Galilee, and casting out demons.
>
> —Mark 1:27, 39, italics mine

> And He was casting out a demon, and it was mute. So it was, when the demon had gone out, that the mute spoke; and the *multitudes marveled.*
>
> —Luke 11:14, italics mine

Deliverance, together with healing, continued throughout Jesus' ministry on the Earth. He came to set the captives free and to liberate those enslaved by demonic powers.

VICTORY OVER PRINCIPALITIES

By triumphing over spiritual rulers and spiritual authorities at the end of His earthly ministry, Jesus fought the ultimate battle:

> Having canceled out the certificate of debt consisting of decrees against us and which was hostile to us; and He has taken it out of the way, having nailed it to the cross. When He had *disarmed the rulers and authorities*, He made a public display of them, *having triumphed over them* through Him. He was conquered by Jesus in His death on the cross, and he was triumphed over.
>
> —Colossians 2:14-15, italics mine

Jesus now sits on the throne in Heaven and intercedes on behalf of His Church. In His waiting for the establishment of the future Kingdom, where Satan and his hosts will be eternally bound, Jesus manifests the wondrous patience of our heavenly Father.

> ...after He had offered one sacrifice for sins forever, sat down at the right hand of God, from that time *waiting* till His enemies are made His footstool.
>
> —Hebrews 10:12-13, italics mine

Sending us into the world to preach the Gospel, Jesus commissioned us to cast out demons, heal the sick, cleanse the lepers and raise the dead—all warfare activities in the terrestrial sphere.

Most assuredly, I say to you, he who believes in Me, the
works that I do he will do also; and *greater works* than
these he will do, because I go to My Father.

–John 14:12, italics mine

When He ascended to the Father, Jesus was given *all* power
over the enemy—in Heaven and on the Earth. Thus empowered,
Jesus transferred the jurisdiction of terrestrial warfare to the Body
of Christ. Therefore, by asking in His name, power is at our
disposal to advance God's Kingdom.

And as you go, preach, saying, 'The Kingdom of Heaven
is at hand.' Heal the sick, cleanse the lepers, raise the dead,
and cast out demons...

–Matthew 10:7-8

Therefore, we have been given authority to aggressively
plunder Satan's kingdom. Jesus has given us divine power to carry
on His ministry and build His Kingdom.

Victorious living in our battles with Satan and his demonic
kingdom is accomplished to the degree that we submit to Jesus'
Lordship. The more we submit every area of our life to Jesus, the
greater the victories we will see. It is yielding to His Lordship and
remaining faithful to His Lordship that brings not only great but
also consistent victories. To be given spiritual authority requires
that we humbly submit to God's authority.

As His followers, we have been given authority to do every
form of terrestrial warfare mentioned in His Word. If a demonic

principality leaves its heavenly arena and manifests on the terrestrial plane, we have authority to rebuke it in Jesus' name. However, if we attempt to make our victory over the enemy more sophisticated by ascending into the second Heaven to contest principalities that rule over geographic regions, then we deviate from the model set forth in Jesus' ministry.

LED TO THE SLAUGHTER

The enemy has lured many into arenas of spiritual combat for which God has not equipped them. Many have discovered that they are left vulnerable and ignorant concerning the enemy who is ready to pounce on them. Some have been stalked and even have become fare fodder for the wicked one.

One lure that Satan uses is false expectations of victory. Excited believers lunge forward onto ground that seems secure, but later proves to be quicksand. As the ground envelopes them, they become paralyzed by fear.

Now, more than ever, we need to remain sober, vigilant, and alert, as the deceitful one, Satan, entices many away from the shores of truth into the depths of deception.

Jesus clearly empowered us to teach and demonstrate all that He did on the Earth (Matthew 28:20). He taught us to love our enemies and to pray for those who persecute us. He taught us to use prayers of repentance and the modeling of His righteousness to destroy the works of the evil one. We are not to contend against flesh and blood, but against spiritual principalities and powers that control the lives of men and women and the world systems against which we all struggle.

Furthermore, we are admonished by Jesus to judge not after the flesh but after the Spirit. It is evil spirits that drive men to do evil things and to make evil decisions. We are to cast out spirits in mankind, *not* in the celestial realm.

Accordingly, Carlos Annacondia from Argentina had a principality appear in his room. He had authority to rebuke the principality because it came into our terrestrial arena, the sphere where Jesus empowered us to extend His Kingdom rule and reign.

When principalities or other demonic beings in the second Heaven invade our earthly realm, we have power to rebuke them. However, we don't have the anointing or the authority to wage war in the heavenly realms. We've only been commissioned to subdue the Earth.

Revealing Flawed Logic

Today, there is some debate on whether believers are authorized to engage in battles in the Heavens. Consider these presuppositions:

Premise 1
Satan's peers in God's original design were all third Heaven hierarchy. Two of his peers were the archangels Michael and Gabriel.

Premise 2

Satan mimics God's authority structure. Therefore, the authority structure of darkness mimics that of Heaven. If this were not so, that would make Satan an originator of design, or in other words, a creator. However, Satan creates nothing. Since there is only one Creator—God —then Satan can only copy, mimic, or counterfeit God's original design and structure.

Premise 3

God's hierarchy is counterfeited in Satan's kingdom. Therefore, for every principality, power, might, and dominion in God's Kingdom, there will be a duplicate principality, power, might, and dominion in Satan's system.

Premise 4

Therefore, for every principality, power, might, and dominion in the third Heaven that blesses geographical areas, there will be the same false authorities in the second Heaven who curse geographical areas.

Premise 5

Only God has power to command His heavenly realms. Therefore, we who at present remain a little lower than the angels ought *not* to presume to command those spiritual beings who are higher ranking in the created order. This includes all of God's heavenly hosts— Michael, Gabriel, or even any lesser angel. Remember,

Gabriel struck Zacharias, the high priest, mute because he spoke presumptively and simply questioned the angel (Luke 1:11-20). If we can't even question angels, why do we think we can speak presumptively to command celestial beings?

Premise 6
Therefore, to presume that we have authority to address Satan's hosts in the second Heaven—except when they leave their assigned abode and transgress into the terrestrial arena—is tantamount to the presumption that we can so address God's third Heaven hierarchy. Such thinking would allow us to command Gabriel and Michael or any other angel to do whatever we want them to do.

Premise 7
Since Scripture is clear that angels only follow commands from God, neither will their counterparts in the second Heaven (i.e., principalities, etc.) respond to our commands. Furthermore, the consequences of such behavior may be grave.

Chapter Seven

Territorial Curses

FROM THE BEGINNING of time, God has allowed principalities and powers to exist around the Earth. Heavenly hosts in the third Heaven exist by God's sovereign will and manifest God's divine decrees. They bring His blessings to mankind.

Principalities in the second Heaven are appointed by Satan and function by his will. Manifesting his decrees, they bring curses upon mankind.

Behold, I set before you today a blessing and a curse: the blessing, if you obey the commandments of the Lord your God which I command you today; and the curse, if you do not obey the commandments of the Lord your God, but

turn aside from the way which I command you today, to
go after other gods which you have not known.
                                    –Deuteronomy 11:26-28

God sends curses upon a nation when mankind fails to
embrace righteousness and instead performs evil acts. Drought
and pestilence ravage the land; foreign armies attack and plunder.

> "I also withheld rain from you when there were still three
> months to the harvest...I blasted you with blight and
> mildew...I sent among you a plague...I overthrew some of
> you; yet you have not returned to Me," says the Lord.
>   –Amos 4:7-11

This was *not* God's perfect will. With regret and long-
suffering patience, God lets mankind reap the consequences of
evil actions, in hope that we will turn and repent. When we
repent of evil and turn toward righteousness, God happily
withholds impending disaster and sends His blessings.

Blessings or curses come from the type of principality that God
has placed or allowed to exist. When mankind changes his actions,
God altars the type of celestial dignitary that rules overhead.

> The instant I speak concerning a nation and concerning a
> kingdom, to pluck up, pull down, and to destroy it, if that
> nation against whom I have spoken turns from its evil, I
> will relent of the disaster that I thought to bring upon it.
> And the instant I speak concerning a nation and

concerning a kingdom, to build and to plant it, if it does evil in My sight so that it does not obey My voice, then I will relent concerning the good with which I said I would benefit it.

–Jeremiah 18:7-10

How does God elevate, demolish, and destroy a nation? Often He allows enemy forces to take them captive. He also does it through famine, drought, war, or even by allowing internal decay and national calamity.

God can soften the severity or change the course of a judgment, if a nation repents and changes its actions. Thus, God brings His blessings or allows curses to afflict the land, depending on the response of people living in the nation.

THE RIGHT TO EXIST

Never does Scripture indicate if you wrestle against a second Heaven principality that God will remove it. Or that by engaging in spiritual warfare and wrestling against a second Heaven principality as an intercessor, you can remove it. If God has allowed a principality to have territorial jurisdiction over a region, then only God can remove the principality. To assault a principality ruling over a geographic region is to engage in warfare against a heavenly authority that God has allowed to have territorial rights of jurisdiction.

REPENTANCE IS THE KEY

This does not mean that we have nothing to do. Repentance is the greatest weapon we have in warfare. It allows God to win the victory for us.

The Bible admonishes Christians to humble themselves, pray, repent, and change their actions. Humble acts move the hand of God. He then removes curses over geographic regions.

> If my people who are called by My name will humble themselves, and pray and seek My face, and turn from their wicked ways, *then I will hear from Heaven, and will forgive their sin and heal their land.*
>   –2 Chronicles 7:14, italics mine

Wisdom from God is consistently characterized by humility. When we humble ourselves before God, He draws near to hear our prayers. When we return to the Lord, He—not we—removes the principality that afflicts the land.

Territorial curses come from lack of repentance. However, when we act in humility, by agreeing with God and repenting for our actions, God removes the affliction. He is compelled by His obedience to His own spiritual laws to remove the curse. Likewise, if enough people *corporately* repent on behalf of a nation for desiring abortion, immorality, or any other number of sinful acts and ask God to remove sin, then He will heal and cast off the intended curse.

IDENTIFICATIONAL REPENTANCE

In repentance and great humility, the prophet Daniel, who was full of extraordinary wisdom and righteousness, took on the priestly function of intercession as a mediator between God and man. In so doing, he identified with the people in his nation and offered prayer on their behalf:

> ...O Lord, great and awesome God, who keeps His covenant and mercy with those who love Him, and with those who keep His commandments, we have sinned and committed iniquity, we have done wickedly and rebelled, even by departing from Your precepts and your judgments.
>
> –Daniel 9:4-5

When Daniel wrote this, Israel was enslaved by the Babylonian empire. A heathen king ruled them. Evil abounded—sexual orgies, abortions, and even child sacrifices were common. However, Daniel did *not* pray against the principality of abortion, child sacrifice, or any other principalities in the demonically ruled kingdom. Nor did he bind the territorial spirits over the nation. Instead, Daniel addressed his prayers to God. His humility and repentance justified God to send His angels Gabriel and Michael to fight in the Heavens on Daniel's behalf. God once again demonstrated that He controls the Heavens.

On the other hand, if binding heavenly principalities had been essential to victory, Daniel would have realized the need. He would have fought the enemy in the heavenly realms. But he didn't. Instead, Daniel humbled himself, prayed, and asked God to forgive his nation. With keen insight, Daniel recognized that repentance was the key to ending the Babylonian captivity.

In prayerful repentance, Daniel identified with the people who committed such gross offenses. As a national leader with great governmental authority, Daniel repented for the sins of others as if they were his own sins. His actions demonstrated that he recognized God alone could remove the curse—if only the people in the land would change their hearts and repent of their stubborn, rebellious, and sinful ways.

Consequently, territorial principalities can be dislodged in two ways: first, by sufficient corporate repentance. Secondly, when those in authority respond in prayer for their city or region or nation, God will act. This is consistent throughout Scripture and continues even today. Thereby, God continues to follow the protocol He established long ago.

Executive Action

When God's appointed authorities and leaders humble themselves, pray, and repent for the sins of their nation, great power is released. When King Solomon prayed and dedicated the temple, fire came down from Heaven and the glory of God filled the temple (2 Chronicles 6:12-7:1). When the King of Nineveh repented in sackcloth and ashes, the nation also repented and was delivered (Jonah 3:7-10).

When the righteous are in authority, the people rejoice;
but when a wicked man rules, the people groan.

                                                –Proverbs 29:2

Similarly, two pastors with regional oversight were given a vision from the Lord six months before *The Washington Post* launched its investigation of the corruption in former President Nixon's administration. God revealed to these pastors the tremendous pollution and wickedness occurring in the White House. In response, they asked God what to do about the revelation. Surprisingly, God asked them "to say four prayers of repentance every day for six months." They obeyed. At the end of six months, one of Nixon's aides uttered a statement in a press conference that launched the Watergate investigation and exposed dishonesty and criminality at a national level.

What does the Scripture mean that if we pray for those in authority, we will live godly and peaceful lives (1 Timothy 2:1-3)? In response to that question, God opened the eyes of a friend of mine who was driving with his wife through several states. As they drove across a border into a state governed by an unbelieving and immoral governor, it was as though they had driven out of sunlight into a dark cloud. A sense of oppression shrouded them. A short time later, they proceeded into a state governed by a Holy Spirit-filled, righteous man. It was as though they had entered into a field of light. Oppression lifted and joy bubbled up within them. Later, the wife had fallen asleep and their route eventually curved back into the first state. Instantly she awoke, nauseated, and said, "We've gone back into that dark state, haven't we?" Thus, the actions of civil leaders over geographic regions have great consequences for those who live within their borders.

DANIEL'S INTERCESSION

When Daniel prayed (Daniel 9), God moved upon the heart of King Darius of Persia, a wicked king. The angel Gabriel told Daniel:

> In the first year of Darius the Mede, I, even I, stood up to confirm and strengthen him.
>
> –Daniel 11:1

As a result of Daniel's prayers and the angel Gabriel's strengthening of King Darius, God stirred the heart of this heathen monarch to begin rebuilding the temple in Jerusalem. This began during the second year of Darius' reign (Ezra 4:24).

Through repentance that was offered by a leader with civil authority, the strongholds of captivity and suppression were cracked. The Kingdom of God gained a "toe hold" that would eventually triumph over the land.

It is essential to note that in his prayer, Daniel did not assault strongholds or principalities; he simply set his face toward God and made his requests by prayer and supplications on behalf of the nation.

> We have sinned and committed iniquity, we have done wickedly and rebelled, even by departing from Your precepts and Your judgments...We have not obeyed the

voice of the Lord our God, to walk in His laws, which He
set before us by His servants the prophets.

—Daniel 9:5,10

Furthermore, I do not believe Daniel was aware that God
would send Gabriel and Michael to defeat the principalities over
Babylon. Daniel simply saw the need to repent without knowing
the outcome. We need to have a similar attitude of obedience to
God regardless of how He chooses to respond. We never know
when or how God may answer our prayers.

GOD ANSWERS BY LIGHTNING

Several years ago, a Holy Spirit-filled county commissioner
attended a prayer meeting in his church. He was concerned about
a movie that would be shown the following evening at the local
drive-in theatre. In order to attract a crowd for the summer season,
the theatre planned to show the movie classic, *The Exorcist.*

The commissioner stood before the congregation and said,
"As a civil shepherd of God's people in this county, I don't
believe God wants His people to be exposed to the demonic
through that movie. Would you join me in repentance and
intercession for our city?"

As dusk approached the next evening, a long line of cars
waited patiently for the ticket office to open. Suddenly, a storm
arose and a lightning bolt shot from the clouds. It struck the
movie screen and demolished it. The theatre was out of business

all summer! God acted in response to the prayers of repentance led by the man He had placed in authority over the region.

ABRAHAM'S AUTHORITY TO REVERSE THE CURSE

In Genesis 20, Abraham told a half-lie to Abimelech, king of Gerar, saying that Sarah was his sister. In fact, Sarah was Abraham's half-sister, but he concealed the fact that she was also his wife. So, Abimelech took Sarah to be his wife. But before he had consummated the marriage, God spoke to this heathen king in a dream.

"Indeed you are a dead man because the woman you have taken is Abraham's wife," God told Abimelech.

The king responded to God, "Would you destroy a nation even though I am innocent?" Although he was not a Hebrew, Abimelech knew that his actions as a leader would bring about devastating repercussions in his kingdom. God showed mercy and told Abimelech that Abraham, who was a leader among the Hebrews and a prophet, had authority to reverse the curse. Abraham prayed for Abimelech and God healed the people living in the kingdom of Gerar.

TAKING BY FORCE

One definition of sin is "when we attempt to take by force what God would have given by grace." Thereby, we insist on instant or premature gratification, which is also like trying to give birth to a baby in two months instead of nine and resulting in a miscarriage.

Similarly, Jacob stole by force the blessing God would have given by grace (Genesis 27). Salvation by works is another attempt to take by force what God would give by grace.

Likewise, when we attack principalities and resist territorial curses *before* sufficient repentance by those in authority or by corporate entities has enabled God to act by grace, we sin by presumption. In essence, we are trying to take by force what God would have freely given by grace.

Driven By Impatience

In Exodus 23, after telling Moses how He would drive out the inhabitants of the Promised Land and accomplish many great feats, God gave His rationale for an apparent delay in removing the enemy:

> I will not drive them out from before you in one year, lest the land become desolate and the beasts of the field become too numerous for you. *Little by little* I will drive them out from before you, until you have increased and inherited the land.
>
> —Exodus 23:29-30, italics mine

This passage speaks of God's wisdom in timing, of the necessity of maturity, and of increase numerically. What does this say about spiritual warfare? It says that if left to our own understanding, we might try to cleanse the land totally, before it is wise to do so. Other spirits, who are far more wicked, may replace what we might drive out. Perhaps we need to heed the warning, "...lest the beasts of the field [demons and principalities] become too numerous for you."

Impatience can propel us forward, *not* pausing to wait upon God. By taking things into our own hands, we may become like Saul who acted hastily (1 Samuel 13:7-14).

We may want to consider the warning in Proverbs 20:21 that "an inheritance gained hastily in the beginning will not be blessed at the end." Often we want things before we are ready to handle the consequences.

Winning a spiritual war requires fervent and effectual prayers. As I have said earlier, Scripture admonishes us to pray for those around us and for those in authority over us. Our intercessions should encompass the world as well as our city and nation. We should always pray, without ceasing. Our prayers should be modeled after the prayers of Jesus and portray the nature of Jesus.

INTERCEDING FOR OUR COMMUNITIES

Our foremost objective is to worship God and to offer Him thanksgiving and praise. In practicing the presence of Jesus, we seek to commune with God. We seek to abandon and submit our will to God. When we do so, the Lord gives us His mind about how to intercede.

Likewise the Spirit also helps in our weaknesses. For we do not know what we should pray for as we ought, but the Spirit Himself makes intercession for us with groanings which cannot be uttered. Now He who searches the hearts knows what the mind of the Spirit is, because He makes intercession for the saints according to the will of God.

—Romans 8:26-27

A Heavenly Blueprint

Jesus taught His disciples how to pray. He did not criticize all public prayers, but He condemned those that attracted attention. He also discouraged vain, meaningless repetitive prayers that were full of religious piety.

By contrast, Jesus focused on intimacy with God, thus establishing prayer as a form of worship and communion. And He said to petition God for the establishment of His Kingdom on Earth.

In this manner, therefore, pray: Our Father in Heaven, hallowed be Your name. Your Kingdom come. Your will be done on Earth as it is in Heaven...deliver us from the evil one...

—Matthew 6:9-13

When Jesus encouraged His disciples to petition God the Father, He was recognizing God's authority and protection in our lives—to deliver us from the evil one. When we pray, we are entreating God to act on our behalf. By asking God for the arrival of His Kingdom on Earth as it exists in Heaven, we are recognizing that God's will is already being done in Heaven.

By speaking of His will being done in Heaven, I do not mean that it is God's will/desire for Satan to attack us. I believe that God has established a divine judicial order and there are consequences for every action. Although it is not His desire that demonic principalities rule over the land, it is ingrained in His will by allowing mankind to have free will. Thus, we make choices that ultimately end up being blessings or curses.

To attack principalities in the second Heaven is to attempt to answer our own prayers as if God would not answer them for us—trying too soon and unwisely to take by force what God would give by grace.

When the apostle Paul detected Satan resisting God's will and the Kingdom's advancement, he asked Christians to pray that he would have boldness to speak the Word of God followed by signs and wonders. In this manner, the works of Satan would be destroyed. God acted on Paul's behalf. He will do the same for us if we ask.

We need to note that not once did Paul address any second Heaven powers of his day. He did recognize their existence, but he always chose to ask God for strength to overcome them rather than taking them on himself. Should we not do the same?

Throughout Scripture, we are encouraged to pray for the ability to live holy and godly lives, which allows God to advance His Kingdom and hasten His return.

> Therefore, since all these things will be dissolved, what manner of persons ought you to be in *holy conduct and godliness*, looking for and *hastening the coming of the day of God*, because of which the Heavens will be dissolved, being on fire and the elements will melt with fervent heat.
> —2 Peter 3:11-12, italics mine

Those who commit their lives to holiness will be given spiritual authority over the nations (Revelation 2:26b). Spiritual power is directly related to the level of righteousness in which we live.

Our prayers, which ascend before God as incense, hasten His return and advance righteousness over the face of the Earth. Intercession is a powerful tool in warfare.

LIBERATION OF BERLIN

In her bestseller, *The Vision of His Glory*, Anne Graham Lotz wrote eloquently about the role of intercession after World War II. Christians around the world began to pray for the Church behind the Iron Curtain.

> Stories of harassment, persecution, poverty, human rights abuse, and depression slipped through the curtain and over the wall. God's people prayed for Him to intervene and deliver Eastern Europe from the tyranny of atheism and oppression. At times triggered by world events, the prayers

of believers around the world intensified. And in November 1989, the Berlin Wall fell, and the Iron Curtain came tumbling down. There was no logical explanation for this dramatic series of events except that "the bowls full of incense which are the prayers of the saints" had filled up! I wonder whose prayer was the last one to come in before God said, "I have all I need in order to proceed to accomplish my purpose."[15]

John Sandford shared with me about the role of intercession reversing territorial curses in Eastern Europe:

Herr Buecker taught East Germans how to join with West Germans in unity, in repentance and intercessory prayers. One day East Germans suddenly began to come to a church in Leipzig, praying fervently in intercession for their country. This was at great risk, because the Stasi (secret police) were watching and recording. Thousands gathered in the church and throughout the city. Herr Buecker afterwards informed us that a decree came from the government *by mistake*, to open the gate! By the time officials discovered what was happening, it was too late to stop the pendulum of history—it had swung to freedom! The Berlin Wall was torn down. The greatest bloodless revolution in modern history followed, as communism fell out of power, the Soviet Union was dissolved, and—miracles of miracles—Germany was reunited! That is the power of intercessory prayer and spiritual warfare for the nations of the world.[16]

Chapter Eight

Advancing God's Kingdom

OR THOUSANDS OF years, a close connection has existed between prayer, advancing the Kingdom of God, and destroying the works of the enemy. Prayer is indispensable in advancing God's Kingdom. The Church was birthed in an atmosphere of prayer (Acts 2) and flourished, despite great spiritual attack from the enemy.

Incredible spiritual authority has been released on the Earth to destroy the works of the enemy and advance God's Kingdom. Although I am convinced that authority has *not* been given to us to have dominion over any of the heavenly realms, that does not mean that we do not need to have great passion in prayer nor does it mean we do not have an understanding that we are at war.

God has always exercised authority in the Heavens and continues to exercise it today. It's God's arena. As the Sovereign of the universe, God has determined that the gates of Hell will not prevail against what He wants to establish on the Earth.

God promises us divine protection.

I will contend with those who contend with you.

–Isaiah 49:25b

The Lord is faithful and He will strengthen and protect you from the evil one.

–2 Thessalonians 3:3

Demonic principalities can hinder us as they did Daniel (Daniel 10:13). But it is the sins and sinfulness of people that cause our churches to become stagnant and spiritually impotent.

If a church is full of unrepentant sin, spiritual maturity is curtailed. Miracles and conversions may seldom happen even though the hearts of some seem pure and the Word is accurately preached. But as we change our hearts and actions through repentance, aided by discernment of spirits, words of knowledge, prophecies, and revelations, God can reveal to individuals territorial hindrances and stimulate corporate repentances. Is this not a divine strategy to take the Earth for God's glory?

KEYS OF AUTHORITY

In Matthew, Jesus said the following:

And I will give you the *keys* of the Kingdom of Heaven,
and whatever *you bind on Earth* will be bound in Heaven,
and whatever *you loose on Earth* will be loosed in Heaven.
              —Matthew 16:19, italics mine

Keys unlock doors of power and authority. Some theologians
believe that the word *key* is a metaphor for the person of the Lord
Jesus Christ (Revelation 1:18). Others believe it represents the
function of the Holy Spirit.

We must take notice that Jesus descended to obtain the keys to
give to us. We often act as though we must ascend to grasp the keys.
If the keys for taking the Heavens were in celestial places, why didn't
Jesus first ascend to find these keys (Ephesians 4:8-9)? Rather, He
descended into Hell to reclaim keys that belonged on the Earth and
had been taken there by Satan. The keys to the Kingdom are earthly,
not celestial. We must fight *for* the Earth, *on* the Earth.

In the book of Revelation, Jesus possesses the keys of Hades
and death. By His Lordship over life and death, Jesus took captive
Satan's power and authority on the Earth.

I am He who lives, and was dead, and behold, I am alive
forevermore. Amen. And I have the *keys* of Hades and
of Death.
              —Revelation 1:18, italics mine

As the promised Messiah from the tribe of Judah, Jesus holds the key of David.

> The *key* of the house of David I will lay on his shoulder...
> –Isaiah 22:22, italics mine

> And to the angel of the church in Philadelphia write, these things says He who is holy, He who is true, "He who has the *key* of David, and shuts and not one opens."
> –Revelation 3:7, italics mine

During Bible times, a practice existed among the Hebrew people. The father or head of the household carried keys on a rope tied around his waist that unlocked the store rooms within the house. Prior to his death, he would call for his oldest son. In a final act, the father would lay the keys on his son's shoulders, signifying the passing of authority from the father to the son.

What Jesus descended to get, He gave to His disciples. They passed them on to us in compliance with the Great Commission. As followers of Jesus, possessing the keys means that we have been given His authority on the Earth. We have never been given the key to Heaven, only keys to this earthly sphere.

Jesus is the power behind the keys. If He is ignored, overlooked, or denied, then neither Heaven's blessings nor those of Earth can be unlocked for us. By turning over the keys to us, Jesus has released authority to bind and loose on the Earth as we see the Father already doing in Heaven.

BINDING AND LOOSING

Some people believe the passage in Matthew 16 suggests if you bind on the Earth, it is subsequently bound in the Heavens. But actually, the reverse is true.

Linguistic studies reveal that the verb in Matthew 16:18-19 is in the future perfect passive periphrastic tense. This simply means that the literal way the verse should read is: "...whatever you bind on Earth *will have already been bound* in Heaven, and whatever you loose on Earth *will have already been loosed* in Heaven." Many Bible publishers include this as a note in the margins.

So, to be more accurate, binding or loosing is *first* done in Heaven, and then manifested on Earth. God binds in Heaven, which allows us to bind on the Earth. God looses in Heaven, so we loose on Earth. This understanding also parallels the prayer example of Jesus in Matthew 6—"on Earth as it is in Heaven." God binds or looses in Heaven depending on the actions of men.

Binding means to prohibit or forbid. *Loosing* means to allow freedom.[17] We watch what God the Father is doing and then bind or loose what He has already bound or loosed.

However, in the context of Matthew 16 and later in Matthew 18, binding and loosing are terms used to describe church discipline—excommunicating or reconciling a sinner. Therefore, we cannot use these passages to support the idea of binding celestial powers.

It is clear in Matthew 18 that following the protocol established by God allows us to walk in authority over the earthly demonic realm. However, there is *no* scriptural precedent for saying, "I bind you, Satan." Even Jesus did *not* speak to Satan that way. Binding Satan is yet to be accomplished by Jesus at the end:

> Then I saw an angel coming down from Heaven, having the key to the bottomless pit and a great chain in his hand. He laid hold of the dragon, that serpent of old, who is the Devil and Satan, and *bound him for a thousand years*; and he cast him into the bottomless pit, and shut him up, and set a seal on him, so that he should deceive the nations no more till the thousand years were finished. But after these things he must be released for a little while.
>
> –Revelation 20:1-3, italics mine

In Scripture, we have a clear example of how to deal with demons when they manifest. We cast them out. Breaking the power of the devil is *best* accomplished by doing the works of Jesus.

We are to fight second Heaven principalities and powers the same way Jesus and His followers did. Jesus Himself said that He only did that which He saw His Father doing. Therefore, if Jesus saw God heal someone in Heaven—perhaps in a vision while He was praying—then power was loosed on Earth to accomplish what He had seen in Heaven.

Although God's people lived under demonic principalities of religion, sexual perversion, and other dark powers, and legions of spirits were spread over the entire Roman Empire, Jesus *never* addressed them in the second Heaven. He only addressed them terrestrially, by ministering to men, women and children, setting them free.

Think about it. Of all the times Jesus taught His disciples, there is not one illustration in which Jesus or His disciples bound celestial beings in the heavenly realms. But there are hundreds of examples of demonic spirits being bound in individuals. This is terrestrial warfare.

PRINCIPALITIES OVER ISRAEL

If we stop to consider, we would realize that principalities operated over Israel during the time of Jesus. Rome and the rest of the known world were driven by principalities of darkness. Jesus never attacked them. Why? As fully man and fully God, Jesus demonstrated man's response to Satan's kingdom. Man was to exercise authority on Earth to defeat the enemy, leaving principalities in the second Heaven to God.

Even when the principalities and powers tried to drown Jesus and His disciples on the Sea of Galilee, Jesus did not speak to the principalities and powers. He rebuked the wind and spoke to the sea (Mark 4:35-41). Jesus' authority over the Earth was greater than Satan's authority. Therefore, He did not have to address the principalities. The Earth responded to a higher authority than the demonic command.

JESUS NEVER LOST HEAVENLY AUTHORITY

The principle Jesus communicated to His followers, just before He ascended to the Father, is *vitally* important to the perpetuation and advancement of God's Kingdom:

> And Jesus came and spoke to them, saying, '*All authority has been given to Me in Heaven and on Earth.* Go therefore and make disciples of all the nations, baptizing them in the name of the Father and of the Son and of the Holy Spirit, teaching them to observe all things that I have commanded you; and lo, I am with you always, even to the end of the age.' Amen.
>
> —Matthew 28:18-20, italics mine

To paraphrase, Jesus said that He had regained all earthly authority. Whatever mankind needed to subdue the Earth which was lost in the Fall, Jesus restored to us. Now, we are to do everything Jesus taught us to do, and to teach others to do likewise. God's Kingdom power will accompany us until He returns.

Remember, Jesus was not saying He had retrieved heavenly authority, because as I said previously, He had never lost it. He was simply stating that He now has *both* authority on Earth as well as in Heaven. What Jesus did not do was as vitally important as what He did.

DON'T FOCUS ON THE GIANTS

When I travel to various cities around the world, people often ask me if I have discernment about principalities and powers over their cities. In trying to grow their church or launch an evangelism initiative, they want to do everything to eliminate the assaults of the enemy.

To their surprise, I tell them I don't even concern myself with the principalities and powers in the Heavens. The shock on their faces reveals what they have been thinking and doing. Instead, I ask if they know what God is going to do in their city. Then, I gently tell them that my focus is on God and what He is doing and planning to do. I do not focus on Satan or his hordes.

When the twelve spies returned to Moses after scouting out the Promised Land, ten focused on the giants (Numbers 13). Two spies, Joshua and Caleb, focused on taking the land and gave a favorable report (Numbers 14:6-9). Joshua and Caleb said "If the Lord delights in us, then He will give us the land. Don't fear the giants in the land. The Lord is with us!" Our question should be, "Is the Lord with us?" If He is, then the giants should fear us.

All too often, we focus on celestial giants instead of concentrating our efforts on taking the land and obtaining the new wine, and its milk and honey. Frequently, I hear people say, "The reason we can't go in is the giants. We must first take them down." I think perhaps a major reason we are not going in to possess the land is that we are more interested in giants than we are desperate to taste the honey of our inheritance.

SEEK GOD'S HEART

Everything I do is to seek to know God's heart, to learn what revelations or miracles He wants to accomplish. And then I try to participate with Him in advancing the Kingdom of God.

Spending time to discern and map the names of demonic principalities that oversee cities and nations only serves to distract me. I am not saying that it has no value, but only that it distracts me from my focus on God and His grand design.

Over the years, I've discovered a simple truth: whatever you focus upon, you steer toward. If you are driving your car around a curve and you focus on a wall as you're driving, most likely you'll hit the wall. But if you quit looking at the wall and focus ahead, you will avoid smashing your car. Whatever you fix your attention upon will consume you. It's true in the natural and in the spiritual.

Likewise when I enter a city, I ask God to reveal His purposes and plans for that church, city or region. If for some reason I discern specific demonic strongholds, then I know that God is going to bring freedom to some people who are harassed by those demonic spirits. However, I don't bind those celestial beings in the heavenly realms. If we seek God, pray, and humble ourselves, then God will bring freedom and deliverance. Furthermore, incredible signs and wonders will usually follow the preaching of God's Word.

I refuse to focus on the evil one. Instead, I choose to focus on God and what He is doing.

John Sandford has also shared about the need to focus on God's purposes and not the enemy's schemes:

Years ago, when Paula and I would see by the Holy Spirit whatever demonic oppressions lurked over the conference site or the region, we would think, "Oh, no, it's going to be tough to minister here." Then it would be, because that was the level of our faith. We were celebrating the strength of the flesh and of the demonic principality, rather than Jesus. The Lord said, "John and Paula, you carry within you an overcoming atmosphere. I live in you and I am stronger than anything in the world. Focus on Me and serve others. I will change the atmosphere for you." God instructed us to read Psalm 84:5-7. From then on, whenever we saw oppressive forces over a church or a region, we would pray, put our faith in His power, and serve–forgetting about those evil forces. Ministry invariably became easier and miracles followed. God did not tell us to be sure to dispose of powers of darkness in the heavenly realms so that we could minister freely. He only reminded us to believe that by His power on and around us, we would turn dry valleys into springs, and would go from strength to strength. Ministry has been a joy ever since.[18]

What is your focus? Discerning dark powers? Wrestling with demonic principalities over your city? Often such concentration tends to intensify warfare, brings depression, and generates demonic activity by giving the enemy a stage on which to perform.

God never instructs us to be concerned about or assault demonic principalities in the second Heaven that afflict geographic areas.

THE LOOK OF LOVE

Scripture encourages us to focus our attention on Jesus, who is altogether lovely, true, noble, just, pure, virtuous, and praiseworthy. He has a good report. Through Jesus, we can take the land, in spite of the giants! Moreover, Jesus has made us kings and priests to serve God eternally (Revelation 1:6).

Jesus has delegated divine authority to us to extend and administrate God's rule on the Earth. This involves confronting dark powers, bringing deliverance and increasing the expectation to see the miraculous works of God.

We do this as a kingdom of priests, embracing a spirit of worship directed toward God. Worship is foundational to advancing the Kingdom of God. It is giving focused attention to God, and requires that we fix our eyes on Jesus (Hebrews 12:2). It is Satan who desires to steal our attention away from Jesus.

Frankly, my determined focus is to seek first the Kingdom of God and His righteousness, humble myself, and pray. I also focus on my need to live a holy life unto God and to pursue peace.

God's Word speaks of humbling ourselves before our Creator and one another. If we do, Scripture promises all these things will be given to us. Embracing a posture of humility and repentance will alter the atmosphere around us. God dwells with those who are contrite and humble (Isaiah 57:15; 66:2). We need to seek His face. He will govern the cosmos. God allows angelic principalities to exist over geographic regions as a blessing and He allows demonic principalities to exist over geographic regions as a curse.

As Graham Cooke, an overseer of a large network of churches in England, has aptly said, "True spiritual warfare is not binding and loosing the enemy, but knowing the majesty and supremacy of God."[19]

Granted, Satan and his demonic kingdom will continue to resist and strike aggressively against God's Kingdom on the Earth. And we will need to rally toward the fight. But our ever-wise Commander, the Lord of Hosts, has drawn the battle lines and established the rules of engagement. To venture beyond our protected realm leaves us vulnerable to vicious attack.

When we abandon our God-given sphere of authority and engage in second Heaven warfare, we stray into a deadly realm where we have no protection or authority, a realm where God never intended His children to be.

SONS OF SCEVA

Nearly two thousand years ago, the seven sons of Sceva violated this fundamental principle of operating without God-given authority:

Then some of the itinerant Jewish exorcists took it upon themselves to call the name of the Lord Jesus over those who had evil spirits, saying "We exorcise you by the Jesus whom Paul preaches." Also there were seven sons of Sceva, a Jewish chief priest, who did so. And the evil spirit answered and said, "Jesus I know, and Paul I know; but who are you?" Then the man in whom the evil spirit was leaped on them, overpowered them, and prevailed against them, so that they fled out of that house naked and wounded.

–Acts 19:13-16

Demonstrating presumption, these men attempted to cast out demons without receiving God's authority. Consequently, the demons subdued, overwhelmed, and wounded the men, who ran for their lives. Perhaps we should heed this example as a warning to the Body.

Chapter Nine

Wisdom for Engaging the Enemy

BEFORE CREATION, a colossal spiritual battle raged. From the Heavens, Satan masterminded war against God and His people—to topple governments and unleash epidemics globally.

On the Earth, Satan's evil minions have eroded value systems, kindled lust and greed deeper and deeper into the hearts of men and women, and killed with viciousness the poor and the oppressed. They operate shrewdly and secretly. Often without realizing it, people grant inroads to the devil, and become ensnared in a lifestyle of deception and destruction.

It's an epic struggle of *win and lose,* which the Kingdom of God will eventually transform to good—weaknesses to strengths, deserts to gardens (2 Corinthians 12:4; Isaiah 51:3). As the firestorm rages on the Earth, Christians have a mandate to fight the realm of darkness and advance the Kingdom of God.

But the question remains: How do we fight a powerful, cunning, and invisible foe? We need to know our enemy. We ought not to remain ignorant of his schemes (2 Corinthians 2:11).

RESISTING THE EVIL ONE

We also need to keep ourselves from falling. We should build ourselves up in faith, pray in the Spirit, and keep fervent our passion for God (Colossians 3:5-17). And we need to be strong in the Lord.

> Finally, my brethren, be strong in the Lord and in the power of His might. Put on the whole armor of God, that you may be able to *stand* against the wiles of the devil. For we do not wrestle against flesh and blood, but against principalities, against powers, against the rulers of the darkness of this age, against spiritual hosts of wickedness in the heavenly places. Therefore, take up the whole armor of God, that you may be able to *withstand* in the evil day and having done all, to stand. *Stand* therefore, having girded your waist with truth, having put on the breastplate of righteousness, and having shod your feet with the preparation of the gospel of peace; above all, taking the shield of faith with which you will be able to quench all the fiery darts of the wicked one. And take the helmet of salvation, and the *sword* of the Spirit,

which is the word of God; praying always with all prayer
and supplication in the Spirit, being watchful to this end
with all perseverance and supplication for all the saints– and
for me, that utterance may be given to me, that I may open
my mouth boldly to make known the mystery of the gospel,
for which I am an ambassador in chains; that in it I may
speak boldly, as I ought to speak.

–Ephesians 6:10-20, italics mine

How do we remain strong and resist the attacks of the
enemy? We must stand against the enemy's deceitful schemes.

To *stand* means to take a firm, defensive position and remain
steadfast. In combat, it's an aggressive defensive posture taken by
someone to ward off blows from an enemy who is trying to take
their land, much like Eleazar did when he fought for David over
a piece of ground full of barley. Eleazar's people stationed
themselves in the middle of the field and defended it until the
Lord brought about a great victory (1 Chronicles 11:14-15).

So when the enemy is poised to fight, we are to resist his
temptations and schemes, and remain steadfastly devoted to Jesus.
To *stand* also means to guard ground that we have already taken, so
that the enemy does not make new inroads into our territory.

To *withstand* means to endure or persevere through long-
term and large-scale conflicts. When under attack from enemy
forces, we continually deflect attacks. It's a relentless war; the
enemy is always attacking. As a Christian, you can withstand the
enemy's attacks because you know that it is God who leads you in
triumphant victory.

Don't Be Deceived

In this fight, we do *not* wrestle against flesh and blood, even though we are contending with people, who are flesh and blood. Men and women are *not* our problem. Instead, we wrestle against demonic forces who capture minds and control the actions of individuals. These evil emissaries create strongholds or fortresses in the ideologies, values, and actions of people around the world.

The verses in Ephesians 6 describe unseen spiritual powers that operate through the people whom we face daily. The apostle Paul, when writing about how we can resist Satan's attacks, encouraged us not to become confused and angry at flesh and blood, but rather to wage war against the demonic spirits who may be driving a person. This is how we are to exercise the authority we were given over demonic principalities and powers.

Scripture implores us not to fight *against* people. Instead, being filled with the Holy Spirit, we battle demonic spirits that operate *through* people. Understanding this, we are enabled to love and pray for others with great compassion, because we understand that it is the enemy who is harassing them. In essence, this is what Paul was referring to when he said that we war against celestial principalities and powers.

Shielding Ourselves

This passage in Ephesians also mandates that we are to quench the fiery darts of the wicked one by deflecting them, protecting ourselves with the shield of faith. We need to guard our minds against fear and unbelief. Using the shield of faith implies possessing a constant and unflinching attitude of faith. We need to cling to God's Word, especially IIis promises, in order to overcome our adversary.

TWO TYPES OF SWORDS

The word *sword* in Scripture, both in the Greek and Hebrew, refers to one of two types of swords. The short sword, which is the length of a forearm, is used only in hand-to-hand combat. Its intent is to mutilate and immobilize the enemy—then to kill him.

Throughout Scripture, swords used by humans were *always* the short sword. The use of this sword in Scripture implies arming oneself with the Word of God to cut through the enemy's thoughts and deceptions that operate through people. It also implies that the enemy is a short distance away, suggesting terrestrial warfare. The Greek word for the short sword is the one used in the Ephesians 6 passage as well as in Hebrews 4:12. The sword is employed to penetrate through people's demonic defenses, prick their consciences, and loose them from their tormentors by thwarting demonic assignments against them.

The second type of sword, a long sword, is mentioned in Genesis 3:24 and Revelation 19:15. This sword extends the length of the body. A devastating first-strike weapon, this sword is used in long-distance fighting. In Scripture, *only* Jesus and His angels wielded the body-length sword. It implies that the enemy is a long distance away, suggesting second Heaven warfare which God does on our behalf. Once again, we see a clear picture of the boundaries God has given us.

Some would say, "I am not trying to ascend into the Heavens. I just want to fire an effective cannon from here to there." But we do not see ascending or firing cannons modeled by Jesus.

THE CUTTING EDGE

Ephesians 6 says the sword of the spirit is the "word of God," which is the Greek word, *rhema*. A rhema word is an utterance of God that has cutting power. It is clearly identified as our short sword. The rhema word, therefore, assists us in defending ourselves from the enemy's attacks and in rightly dividing spiritual issues from soulish issues (2 Timothy 2:15; Hebrews 4:12).

PROLONGED WARFARE

Throughout Ephesians 6, the apostle Paul addressed the need to be prepared for prolonged spiritual conflict and to be knowledgeable about how to engage hostile forces effectively when they manifest through others. This passage is about a fight where the enemy is very close—face-to-face and terrestrially positioned—in which we use the short sword in hand-to-hand combat to resist him.

At first glance, it might appear that Paul is advocating second Heaven warfare in Ephesians 6, but upon closer examination and because Jesus never demonstrated second Heaven warfare, we have to take another look at that passage of Scripture. Paul had a revelation of Jesus; therefore, he would comply with Jesus' teachings.

In Ephesians 6, Paul is actually teaching how to maintain a defensive posture when attacked by principalities and powers in the terrestrial arena.

STRONGHOLDS THAT ENSNARE

As the father of lies (John 8:44), Satan cunningly weaves a web of deceit, distortion, and disinformation that affects our perceptions and our belief systems. He insidiously injects poison into our minds, creating doubts and fearfulness. Much as in a game of chess, if Satan can cause us to focus on the wrong maneuver or objective, especially one that seemingly will cause us harm and weaken us, then he has won the battle. At best, our power is diminished and at worst, we die.

In a related passage in 2 Corinthians, the apostle Paul emphasized again that our foe is *not* flesh and blood. Instead, our enemy is a demonic principality that seeks to exalt itself against God and attack through people:

> For though we walk in the flesh, we do not war according to the flesh. For the weapons of our warfare are not carnal but mighty in God for pulling down strongholds, casting down arguments and every high thing that exalts itself

against the knowledge of God, bringing every thought
into captivity to the obedience of Christ.

–2 Corinthians 10:3-5

Since Satan attacks our minds, we are told to pull down
every stronghold and cast down vain imaginations, bringing every
thought into captivity for Christ. If Satan can control our minds,
then he rules our behavior. Therefore, Scripture admonishes us to
renew our minds and resist the enemy:

Do not be conformed to this world, but be transformed by
the *renewing of your mind,* that you may prove what is the
good and acceptable and perfect will of God.

–Romans 12:2, italics mine

Therefore submit to God. *Resist the devil* and he will flee
from you.

–James 4:7, italics mine

FORTRESSES OF THE MIND

The Bible speaks of mental strongholds. Individual mental
strongholds are habitual ways of thinking. When we build a
habitual or practiced way of thinking, it becomes a stronghold in
our minds. Such strongholds have to be recognized, repented of,
and reckoned as dead on the Cross.

Likewise, you also, reckon yourselves to be dead indeed
to sin, but alive to God in Christ Jesus our Lord.

–Romans 6:11

We have to practice filling our minds with virtuous ways of
thinking. Our minds are like computers. We have to reprogram
them (Philippians 4:8-9; Romans 12:2) and engage in spiritual
warfare against our own individual mental strongholds.

We also live in a corporate world. Corporate mental
strongholds are habitual and practiced ways of thinking that
delineate society's mentality. They, too, have a life of their own.
These corporate mental strongholds have a structure forged in the
shared intellect of mankind. These can be expressed as traditions,
philosophies, or mind-sets.

That's why the apostle Paul said not to be taken captive by
philosophy or traditions of men (Colossians 2:8). Philosophy—
the general beliefs, concepts, and attitudes of a group of people—
has the power to drive the actions of people. "As a man thinks, so
he is" (Proverbs 23:7).

To illustrate this point, you may know a couple who are not
getting along. Before long, they may consider divorce. Why?
Principalities have woven a corporate mental stronghold of
divorce over the couple's minds. Therefore, the couple can no
longer think clearly about their children or their vows or
obedience to God. They become self-consumed by the
stronghold that now controls their souls.

Veiled Perceptions

The function of a corporate mental stronghold is to take you captive by placing a veil over your eyes. A corporate mental stronghold operates to blind you, just as Satan has blinded the minds of unbelievers to keep them from seeing the light of the gospel and the glory of Christ Jesus (2 Corinthians 4:4). So, the function of a corporate mental stronghold is to create in you tunnel vision or to obscure and contradict the Word of God by twisting truth and history.

Another function of corporate strongholds is to infiltrate your mind with socially acceptable *buzzwords*. Buzzwords are important-sounding words or phrases that offer little meaning, but they sound logical. They are intended to end discussions or cause surrender to the mind-set of the culture. Here are some in-vogue phrases or buzzwords that you may have heard: "I only have one life to live." "My God wants me to be happy." "Isn't God a god of love?" "God's grace will cover it."

Individual as well as corporate strongholds are wielded by demons who are under orders from principalities and rulers of darkness.

Suppose you are ministering to a couple but nothing seems to penetrate a wall you sense is there. They cannot hear you, because the stronghold operating in them has blinded their minds. That's why spiritual warfare against a stronghold is necessary, in order that the couple can come to their senses.

When you are praying for a person who is demonized, you are fighting a demon who is ruled by a principality. The battle is not a celestial battle but a very earthly one. When you are waging war against a stronghold, you are endeavoring to create a space of time for the person to come to himself or herself. However, there is no guarantee that if that time is created, the person will come to his or her senses. People must make choices by their own free will, and repent of their errant thinking in order to become free.

ARMED WITH REPENTANCE

I believe that if people in a city would gather corporately to repent and to beseech God to remove a principality, God would then set in motion divine acts that would heal the people and the land. Principalities do exist over cities and geographical areas, but wisdom encourages us to address our prayers *to* God and ask Him to deliver us from the evil one.

Several years ago, some intercessors received a vision of a principality called the "empire spirit". This principality could be discerned in pastors who built their spiritual empires, or in business men who built financial empires and ignored their families. Many intercessors began to contend with this spirit. They were warned by a godly prophetic leader first to enlist men and area pastors to help guide them in the repentance process. But the intercessors didn't heed the instruction. A year later, the group, who had a wonderful reputation for being united, agreeable and joyful, began to struggle with power plays inside their group. They began to despise and resent one another. Unknowingly, they now had operating in their midst the very spirit against which they were contending! The empire spirit had blinded them to their own pride and self-sufficiency, and thus, the building of their own personal empires.

OUR SPIRITUAL ARSENAL

John Sandford wrote in his book, *A Comprehensive Guide to Deliverance and Inner Healing*:

> Our weapons—which include the sword of the Spirit, the love of God, the blood of Jesus, the shield of faith, and prayer and repentance—are far more powerful than anything the enemy has. We can destroy every stronghold we encounter, for we battle not with our own strength, but with the weapons of God, eternal and invisible.[20]

I agree with John. If someone curses, slanders, or attacks me, I don't view this as a human attack. I see it as a spiritual attack— one in which demonic spirits have created strongholds in a person's mind. These strongholds instigate harmful behaviors aimed at me. Understanding this helps me seek discernment about what motivates a person. It also encourages me not to retaliate against a person. Instead, by the Holy Spirit, I am able to *bless* the person.

BEWARE OF PRIDE

In a similar manner, Jesus gave His disciples authority over demons that afflict people. He told them to herald the coming Kingdom of God and cast demons out of people, not out of Heaven.

Discovering the results of this newfound jurisdiction over demonic spirits on Earth caused His seventy followers to greatly rejoice. But Jesus cautioned them about becoming prideful or cocky about their authority.

> Then the seventy returned with joy, saying, "Lord, even the demons are subject to us in Your name." And He said to them, "I saw Satan fall like lightning from Heaven. Behold, I give you the authority to trample on serpents and scorpions, and over all the power of the enemy, and nothing shall by any means hurt you. Nevertheless *do not rejoice in this*, that the spirits are subject to you, but rather rejoice because your names are written in Heaven.
> —Luke 10:17-20 italics mine

In this passage, Jesus illustrates spiritual boundaries. Jesus was also communicating that while He had given them authority on Earth, He now had authority in both Heaven and the Earth and used it to remove Satan. Once again, Jesus specifically demonstrated that our authority is over the earthly demonic realm. We have power to trample on serpents and scorpions or any power that manifests itself here on Earth. The examples Jesus used in this passage were of terrestrial spheres of authority and

He used earthly creatures (serpents and scorpions) to illustrate that point.

No doubt, seeing demons shriek and come out of people induced a rush of excitement in the disciples. But Jesus admonished them *not* to rejoice over the fact that demons were subject to them, rather to be glad that their names were written in the Lamb's Book of Life. Jesus knew they were being tempted to become self-confident and full of pride in their newfound anointing.

As with any anointing, we need to be clothed with humility, since God resists the proud (1 Peter 5:5). God hates pride. It led to Satan's downfall. Being deluded by pride can cause us to celebrate our own self-importance.

Chapter Ten

Practical Guidelines for Warfare

IF YOU FIND yourself in extended and prolonged spiritual warfare, there are a number of prerequisites that need to happen.

First, get clear guidance from the Holy Spirit. Ask Him if you should go into spiritual warfare. Is this something God wants you to do or are you simply responding automatically to a need that you have discerned? Do you tend to be a rescuer? Do you have an automatic need to rescue? God is the only rescuer. If you try to take His place, both you and the person you are trying to rescue will drown.

Second, spiritual warfare over geographical regions or churches is won by armies, not by individual heroes. Don't be a lone ranger. Recruit others to join you in repentance, fasting, and prayer. It took masses of people acting unrighteously to create the stronghold now manipulated by the principality. It will take a number of people responding righteously to reverse Satan's legal jurisdiction.

Third, be diligent to maintain a prayer vigil and persevere in intercession with God. It's easy to become discouraged when we pray for others. Results can seem slow in coming, but Jesus urges us to be persistent, to remain in an attitude of prayer, and not to lose heart (Luke 18:1-8).

As you engage in spiritual warfare, here are some additional guidelines that may be helpful:

1. HIDE YOURSELF IN GOD

When we engage in spiritual warfare at any level, we become exposed to the sight of the powers of darkness. Normally we are hidden in Christ Jesus (Colossians 3:3). Psalm 91 says that God has given His angels charge over us, to keep us in all our ways. However, when we are asking God to dispose of a principality, we become known to the intelligence network of darkness. We have opened a door and we can attract demonic powers that launch a counterattack against us. Therefore, we need to know how to say *hiding* prayers.

Hiding prayers are those that enable us to maintain a "stealth" position in prayer. The stealth bombers of the U.S. Air Force provide a good analogy. As we pray for protection and hide ourselves in Jesus, He deflects our enemy's "radar" and we remain unseen. We need to pray to obscure all the pathways over which the enemy has access to us. When combined with repentance, such prayers hide from the enemy our failures and shortcomings, and place a protective cloud around us so that the enemy cannot legally penetrate and cause us harm.

Each day I pray: "Lord, I've been exposed. Hide me, my wife, my children, my friends, and relatives so that Satan cannot attack through any loophole or any person."

However, saying hiding prayers when we have been presumptive, and have not fought by God's commands or within His authority structure, may not be very effective because presumption pulls us out from underneath God's umbrella of protection.

2. Expect Counterattacks

In spiritual warfare, the enemy will mount counterattacks. Expect the enemy to launch attacks through every open door he finds in our lives. We must avert and withstand the enemy's retaliatory strikes.

Jesus said that if you are going to see faults in another, first take the plank out of your own eye before you take the speck out of your brother's eye. This provides protection, because if you pray about anything in someone else, Satan will counterattack by hitting you in the same area.

In counterattacks, the first line of defense is to do what Jesus said—to take up your Cross (Matthew 11:38). If you are praying for a stronghold of lust over a friend, then you must go to the Lord and ferret out any lust in your own life. If you engage in spiritual warfare for lust operating in a person, and you begin to feel lust, you may need cleansing in this area as well.

Ministry to others in spiritual warfare is thus a tremendous blessing. It forces us to see our own sin and die more quickly to ourselves. Turn what the enemy has meant for harm into good by using the enemy's counterattack to discover in yourself what *still* needs to be crucified on the Cross. Scripture says wisdom is a protection to the person who has it (Proverbs 3:21-23).

Knowing that you will confront a counterattack should become part of your preparation, so that you will not be blindsided by the enemy. Remain aware and alert so that when the counterattack comes, you are ready to deal with it. Realizing that counterattacks will come enables you to be prepared to recognize thoughts or actions that you would not normally think of as demonic attacks. For instance, when someone insults you, you won't be so inclined to take it personally.

Ask God to reveal to you the area(s) that haven't yet died in your life. The more you bring these to the light of Christ, that practice will become your best defense from counterattacks.

If God calls you to be a warrior in a given situation, then He knows that you need to face the same issue in your own life (1 Corinthians 1:26). If you were called to do warfare, it may be because you're weak, not because you are strong. The best way to deal with the enemy's counterattack is by agreement, "Lord, it *is* in me. Bring it to death on the Cross." There is security in the Cross of Jesus. There is no security in denial.

3. GATHER OTHERS AROUND YOU

Spiritual warfare is to be conducted by armies, *not* solitary exposed heroes. It takes corporate prayers and repentances to dislodge principalities over areas, such as cities, states, and nations. Lone-ranger intercessors endanger themselves and their groups. An army must repent for the sins of their fathers that allowed the attack to legally come. For example, suppose that the Lord tells me there is a principality over Dallas that is named *Greed.* If I attack that principality, I am in presumption. I am like a sergeant who is trying to capture a hill that the general didn't tell me to take. By doing that, I expose the larger body of troops—the flank—to attack by the enemy. If I am going to do that kind of warfare in Dallas, then I need to talk to all the pastors and prayer groups of the area and make them aware of the name of the principality and ask that we all join in repentance for greed.

Repentance from our sins and those of our forefathers is the most powerful weapon we have in spiritual warfare. It removes the legal ground that Satan has taken. God may reveal the principalities over cities, but there is a right way to fight them. The right way is petitioning God to remove them and repenting of that which allowed the demonic spirit rulership.

If there is no repentance to replace the vacuum left by the demon, it has permission to return. When he does, he will look to see if the person or area is occupied by the Lord. If they are not, he and seven worse spirits will come back, and the city or region is worse than it was at the beginning (Matthew 12:43-46).

When you are engaging corporate mental strongholds over cities or regions, armies of intercessors are needed. Through repentance, you need to ask for a corporate love, a corporate unity, a corporate bond of peace, and a corporate spirit of generosity to fill the people in a city or region. Thus, God is justified in removing the evil rulers placed there by Satan.

4. GET CONFIRMATIONS

Guidance must be clearly received and carefully checked by the wise within the Body. There needs to be confirmation, lest we rush in where angels fear to tread and act presumptuously.

Be careful about getting confirming signs from your friends. They will probably like you too much to disagree. Confirming signs should come from an independent source that is well established in the Lord. Satan can send a dark angel to give you confirming signs.

There was a time when I thought the Holy Spirit was convincing me to pray a certain way so I could defeat the enemy. I began to command and bind principalities over geographic areas. I would, with great passion, command these powers to be broken. Shortly after I began to do this, Satan stopped his attack on my life, which convinced me that I had power and that what I was doing was working. Later, when the Lord gave me the *Hatchets at the Moon* dream (page 13), I saw that it was a delusion and Satan was actually luring me deeper into his trap. I had swallowed the hook, thinking I was hooking him.

Satan can bully us into fighting him. His tactics are called wiles—beguiling or playful tricks (Ephesians 6:11). He can withdraw his attack to convince you that you're on the right track, when you're not. He can work signs and wonders. Satan is willing to lose a few battles in order to win a war.

Pool hall hustlers use a similar scheme. They lose the first game or two and then beg you to play again to give them one or more chances to recoup their losses. The naïve player agrees, expecting to increase his earnings, when in fact, he has been set up for a big financial loss.

Many people have gotten into spiritual warfare and had some successes, which convinced them their methods were correct. Then, the enemy attacked viciously.

5. SAY CLEANSING PRAYERS

When we enter into spiritual warfare we may become defiled and surrounded by demons. This is especially true if you are praying for someone who has a mental stronghold of a spirit of lust. If you have a burden bearing nature, you may be identifying with a person as an intercessor. The person's lust may lodge in you, take root and eventually defile you. From any spiritual encounter, it is possible to be "slimed" with demonic spirits that operate in others.

Therefore, we must say *cleansing* prayers daily. We need to ask God to wash away and cleanse us from every defilement that we received, whether human or demonic. Reading the Bible so as to be washed by the water of the Word is a great way to be cleansed (Ephesians 5:26).

6. REPAIR YOUR ARMOR

Satan's attacks can harm and possibly invalidate your ministry. You can expect any area in your life that is unsanctified to be hit with a flaming dart of the enemy. In one sense, you can rejoice because through that God can reveal to you what has not been brought to Him. If you want to find out what has not been dealt with in your life, simply minister to someone else. God will show you.

You may want to ask God to reveal any area in your life that is a gaping hole—any possible hidden motive—in relation to others. Often we don't see our weaknesses. Give to others the right to examine your life and speak truth to you (Ephesians 4:15). The best preparation for warfare is to commit to a group and let the group begin to examine you to find the areas that are hidden. In this, we do not want to become naval-gazers. But we want to give the Lord opportunity to reveal in us what needs to be exposed, for our own protection and sanctification (Romans 15:14; 1 Corinthians 12:25; Ephesians 4:2).

Before Jesus began His ministry, He entered into forty days of prayer and fasting. I believe one aspect of Jesus' prayer and fasting was to ask God to reveal any area in which He could be tempted before He began His ministry.

Putting on the armor of God is a poetic way of saying, "I choose to examine anything in my life that is impure."

7. ALWAYS SHOW COURTESY

We do not win the battle by becoming like the enemy. We should heed Michael's example and the warning in Jude 9 not to revile.

In delivering a demonized person, we should not call the devil "slewfoot," "slimy serpent," or some other odious name. The hallmark of Jesus' Kingdom is courtesy. You do not win against Satan by using his tactics.

Remember in *Star Wars*, Luke Skywalker, who dreamt of becoming a Jedi, had an argument with his father who had embraced the dark side of his anger and thus had become Darth Vadar. In a sword fight, the devilish ruler of the empire encouraged Luke to let go and release his anger, because if Luke would fight with anger and venom, then Luke would have chosen the dark side.

Similarly, I've watched too many intercessors inadvertently scorn God's creation by the way they passionately attack celestial dignitaries.

8. OFFER YOUR STRATEGIES TO GOD

Knowledge and strategies can be helpful. But knowledge can become an "Ishmael" if you don't put it on the altar. The striving after knowledge may cause you to err in Gnosticism—elevating the role of knowledge in pursuit of spiritual warfare victories. You may be seeking knowledge rather than seeking Jesus. Furthermore, you may be relying on your strategy rather than on the Holy Spirit's strategy.

9. Pick Your Battles

Spirits such as homosexuality, abortion, and divorce are too large and ancient for us to defeat alone. Nor does God call us to attack them. But we are called to wrestle against these things in relation to individuals and groups.

If you perceive a stronghold of homosexuality which blinds and controls an individual for whom you are called to intercede, and if God so commands, you can bind that stronghold over that individual's mind. However, do not cast out a stronghold. An individual or corporate mental stronghold is flesh. You do not cast flesh out. You take flesh to the cross by repentance.

In such a case, you are fighting for a space of time in which a person can come to his senses. Remember the prodigal son when he had fallen under the stronghold of riotous living. His father was praying, and the Scripture says that the son "came to himself" and returned home (Luke 15:17). His right mind was returned to him.

You will know when your prayers have begun to take effect. The individual will begin to see and to think more clearly. The person will no longer block and twist what is said. The person will begin to understand and state some of the things he or she is up against. Hence, the reign of denial in the person's life will have been broken.

10. Live a Balanced Life

If spiritual warfare is the only thing you do, it's inevitable that it will become your identity and eventually an idol in your life. Be sure to balance your activities. Take walks and get exercise. Venture into nature. Alternate your activities. Play games. Get enough sleep. Eat right. You will not lose spiritual power. Instead, you will recharge your batteries and find renewed strength to soar with God.

Regularly set aside time for worship and communion. Keep a personal Sabbath. Abide in the presence of God, and gaze on the beauty of His holiness. Cultivate a mind-set of internal stillness and rest, thus developing greater intimacy with God. Celebrate communion with Him.

11. CULTIVATE THE ART OF LISTENING

Because it's so important, I repeat, give others authority to speak into your life and to give you warning when you are manifesting the spirit against which you are fighting. Listen to their corrections and reprimands.

Do not get isolated from your family and friends. Give your spouse and friends the right to challenge you and examine you. When they point out your weaknesses, hear them. Scripture says those who hate reproofs will die and those who hear rebukes are wise (Proverbs 9:8-9; 10:17; 12:1).

Be willing to hear correction, especially from young believers (Psalm 8:2). Often, God will use the least likely person—even your enemies—to correct you. He may even speak through a donkey to cure a warring madness (Numbers 22:22-35).

Chapter Eleven

Prayers of the Saints

The Lord Jesus Christ finds His highest glory in intercession—a way of selfless prayer that involves demonstrating love for others. Even now, He sits at the right hand of God interceding for us (Romans 8:34). Like Melchizedek, the Bible says that Jesus lives to make intercession for us (Hebrews 7:25). Jesus also said, "My house shall be a house of prayer" (Luke 19:46).

As His friends, we are invited to join Him as He opens the door and gives us access into the court of Heaven. We have the honor and privilege of presenting our prayers on behalf of others before the Maker of the universe.

Wonderful results are promised to us. Jesus said that if we abide in Him and if His words abide in us, we can ask whatever

we wish and it will be done, so that our joy may be complete
(John 15:7; 16:24).

EXHORTATION TO INTERCESSION

Blow the trumpet in Zion, consecrate a fast, call a sacred
assembly; gather the people, sanctify the congregation,
assemble the elders, gather the children and nursing babes;
let the bridegroom go out from his chamber, and the bride
from her dressing room. Let the priests, who minister to
the Lord, weep between the porch and the altar; let them
say, "Spare Your people, O Lord," and do not give Your
heritage to reproach, that the nations should rule over
them. Why should they say among the peoples, 'where is
their God?' Then the Lord will be zealous for His land, and
pity His people.

–Joel 2:15-18

Therefore He is also able to save...those who come to God
through Him, since He always lives to make intercession
for them.

–Hebrews 7:25

Let us therefore come boldly to the throne of grace, that we
may obtain mercy and find grace to help in time of need.

–Hebrews 4:16

THE PRIVILEGE OF INTERCESSION

Intercessory prayer is God's ordained way of allowing us the privilege of co-laboring with Him (Hebrews 4:16). Grace and mercy are given as our privileged portion (Isaiah 30:18-23).

THE PURPOSE OF INTERCESSION

Prayer was to be the power by which the Church manifested the Kingdom of God on the Earth (Jeremiah 33:3). Oftentimes, a lack of prayer is a reason we lack power over our nation (Isaiah 43:22). Jesus has given to us the weapon of prayer in order that we will be empowered to demonstrate the works of His Kingdom on the Earth. Prayer opens the doorway for God to manifest miracles, healing, deliverance, restoration, and signs and wonders (Luke 11:13).

When we pray, our foremost prayer should be for a greater release of the Holy Spirit upon the Church worldwide. God's release of the Holy Spirit is inseparably connected to us asking for it (Isaiah 32:11-15).

Jesus admonished His disciples to pray always with persistence (Luke 18:1). During His days on the Earth, He offered prayers with loud cries and tears (Hebrews 5:7) and with great earnestness (Luke 22:44).

For this reason we are to stir ourselves up, gather, train, and band together as many as we can to be God's reminders (Isaiah 62:1-2, 6-7). Only intense, persevering prayer overcomes worldliness and unrighteousness, both inside and outside of the Church. Furthermore, it involves the following:

Praying fervently–James 5:16
Praying persistently–Luke 11:8
Praying purely–Psalm 24:3-4
Praying faithfully–Luke 18:8

We need apostolic power so that the Word can pierce the hearts of the hearers (Acts 2:37; Hebrews 4:12), ignite the fire that consumes the hearts of the hearers (Zechariah 12:6), and shatter the hearts of the hearers (Jeremiah 23:29).

HEALING BALM FOR THE EYES

If you have gifts of intercessory prayer and discernment of spirits, be careful to focus on God and not on Satan and his kingdom. Pray for your communities. Ask God to change the hearts of men and women who live in the land. Ask God to increase acts of righteousness in your cities and to send the spirit of conviction of sin, righteousness, and judgment.

If you can discern spirits that hover over cities, consider rallying others to join you in expressing righteous acts that display the opposite spirit. For example, if you discern that a principality of pride exists in an area, humble yourself and ask God to break the power of pride in your life. Then ask others to join you. It's God who turns the principalities of curses into heavenly blessings.

If you have engaged in second Heaven warfare and have undergone vicious attacks by the enemy, you may want to repent of violating God's authority structure. Ask God to break off the demonic attack and give you further insight into realms of spiritual authority. Humbly ask God to heal your wounds and to protect you so that you don't fall prey to the diversions and schemes of the enemy, further enabling him to harm you, your family, or your church.

Coming to God as little children and humbly asking for His mercy will bring forth healing. God yearns to father us and teach us His ways. He longs to heal us, so that the Word of God will spread in our hearts and lives. As a result, Jesus will be exalted.

SUGGESTED PRAYERS

As Jesus calls you deeper into intercession, here are some suggestions that may be helpful to you. Many of these have evolved from my personal devotional life. I offer them as seed for further contemplation and prayer.

IN PERSONAL DEVOTIONS

1. Pray that your prophetic and intercessory gifts will portray the testimony of Jesus (Revelation 19:10).

2. Pray that you will be *filled* with the spirit of

wisdom and revelation in the knowledge of God (Ephesians 1:17).

3. Pray that your eyes of understanding will be *enlightened* and that you will know the hope of your calling in Jesus (Ephesians 1:18).

4. Pray that your heart does *not* harden, that your mind and understanding do not become darkened (Ephesians 4:18); and that your emotions do not become impenitent through jaded perceptions or by taking God's glory for granted (Mark 6:52); pray that your soul does not wither by the continued willful commitment of sin (Hebrews 3:15).

5. Pray that you will have *continual* fellowship with God the Father and Jesus Christ through the blessing of the Holy Spirit (Philippians 2:1).

6. Pray in the Spirit often (Romans 8:26-27; 1 Corinthians 14:18-19; Ephesians 6:18; Jude 20).

During Corporate Intercession

1. When we pray corporately, we should *not* go into great detail about our lives and our families. Talk to

God, instead of explaining to others what you mean. Remember to take time to remind God of His promises made in Scripture (Isaiah 62:6-7) and to demonstrate the fullness of your faith and trust in Him.

2. Consider dedicating yourself and asking others to commit to a long-term course of action to fulfill Jesus' exhortation to intercede day and night for the release of His Spirit throughout the Church (Luke 18:7-8).

WHEN PRAYING FOR CHURCHES

We must focus on petitioning God and resist pridefully "preaching to people" in our prayers. A greater release of the Holy Spirit will settle the details of personal obedience in the lives of believers (John 16:8; Acts 9:31; Romans 14:17). Ask God to give His Church a greater release of conviction of sin, judgment, righteousness, peace, comfort, and a greater measure of the fear of God.

1. For times of worship, pray:

- For the presence of God to be powerfully manifested.
- For the glory of God to literally fill the room.
- That God will give manifestations of angelic ministries (Hebrews 1:14).
- For unique and powerful manifestations of the Holy Spirit during worship.

- For the prophetic spirit of God to rest on worship leaders and musicians.

- For clear wisdom and ability to flow with the leading of the Holy Spirit.

- For worshippers to embrace a call to holiness, healed of diseases, refreshed by the Holy Spirit, touched by the power of God, baptized with the Holy Spirit, and set free from demonic spirits.

2. For the times of teaching and preaching, pray:

- That there will be deliverance from sin, from demonization, and from sickness during the teaching time.

- That conviction will rest on the Word to minister salvation to non-Christians and clearer revelation to the Body of Christ.

- That the anointing of the Holy Spirit will powerfully fall during the preaching of the Word.

3. For ministry times, pray:

- For manifestations of the gifts of the Holy Spirit.

- For the Holy Spirit to powerfully heal, encourage, and refresh all believers.

4. In general, you may also want to pray for the following:

- For an anointing that the conviction of sin would fall in the meetings, resulting in evangelism of the lost and the unchurched.

- For radical salvations, healings, and deliverances among the Body of Christ so that we may all walk in greater purity and single-minded devotion to God.

- For a generous spirit of giving that would be evidenced among believers to support greater outreaches to the poor and other various mission opportunities.

- For prosperity to grace those who are out of work and for new opportunities for employment.

CONCLUSION

Our greatest passion and priority should be intercession—the longing of our spirits for God. When prayer is the supreme focus of our hearts, we discover hidden treasures of intimacy with God. Our inner spirits are transformed. And greater revival power is released through us that can potentially sweep millions into the Kingdom of God.

Therefore, keep asking, keep seeking, and keep knocking (Matthew 7:7). God is waiting to hear the prayers of the saints and to unleash the excellent power of His wonderful name on the Earth as it is in Heaven.

Notes

1. Judson Cornwall, *It's God's War: A Biblical View of Spiritual Warfare* (Hagerstown, Md.: McDougal Publishing, 1998), 21. Used with permission.

2. Docestism, which comes from the Greek verb "to seem" is a Gnostic-type heresy that views Jesus Christ as a divine phantom, not a real man. As such, docetics believed that Jesus only seemed to suffer for man's sins since phantoms are incapable of dying. Some taught that a Christ-spirit came upon the man Jesus at the baptism and left Him at the crucifixion. For further reference, see Bruce Shelley, *Church History in Plain Language* (Nashville: Word Publishing, 1995), 50. F. F. Bruce, *The Spread Flame: The Rise and Progress of Christianity from Its First Beginnings to the Conversion of the English* (Grand Rapids: Wm. B. Eerdmans Publishing Company, 1970), 245.

3. Terry Law, *The Truth About Angels* (Lake Mary, Fla.: Creation House, 1994), 167. Used with permission.

4. A religion from Persia, Manichaeans viewed the universe as an eternal conflict between good and evil powers. Like the Gnostics, they taught that Jesus had no material body and

did not actually die. His purpose was to teach men the way out of the kingdom of darkness into the Kingdom of Light. Manichaeans rejected everything that suggested Christ's real sufferings in Scripture and discarded the Old Testament altogether. They also viewed man as a combination of good and evil and his task is to free the good inside him from the evil by prayer and abstinence from riches, lust, wine, meats, luxuries, among other things. For further study, see Bruce Shelley's *Church History in Plain Language*, 125-126.

5. Judson Cornwall, *It's God's War: A Biblical View of Spiritual Warfare* (Hagerstown, Md.: McDougal Publishing, 1998), 52. Used with permission.

6. Leanne Payne, *Listening Prayer* (Grand Rapids: Baker Book House, 1994), 67. Used with permission.

7. *Merriam-Webster's Collegiate Dictionary, Tenth Edition* (Springfield, Mass.: Merriam-Webster, Incorporated, 1998), 1003, 1046.

8. Some early rabbinic leaders believed in the existence of seven Heavens. Many scholars believe the Bible speaks of three Heavens. Scripture speaks of the *third Heaven* which is the dwelling place of God's throne (2 Corinthians 12:2). Scripture also says that Jesus "passed through the Heavens" (Hebrews 4:14). Nehemiah referred to the third Heaven as the *Heaven of Heavens* (Nehemiah 9:6). Many believe that Satan's command post is in the middle Heaven or second Heaven. You can read more about this in D. Douglas et al., *The New Bible Dictionary* (Grand Rapids: Wm. B. Eerdmans

Publishing Company, 1975), 510 and in Terry Law's *The Truth About Angels*, 112.

9. Gnosticism, which appeared in the first few centuries of Christianity, was widely prevalent in the Mediterranean world and embraced the concept of knowledge for its own sake (i.e., knowledge is power). When the teaching was combined with Christian teachings, it had a great allure. But, it minimizes the historical death and resurrection of Jesus Christ. In so doing, it elevates man's knowledge over the finished work of Jesus Christ. You may want to read J. D. Douglas et al., *The New Bible Dictionary* (Grand Rapids: Wm. B. Eerdmans Publishing Company, 1975), 473. Kenneth S. Latourette, *A History of Christianity*, vol. 1 (San Francisco: HarperCollins Publishers, 1975); Vladimir Lossky, *The Mystical Theology of the Eastern Church*, (Greenwood, S.C.: The Attic Press, Inc., 1973); Geoffrey W. Bromiley et al., *The International Standard Bible Encyclopedia*, vol. 2 (Grand Rapids: William B. Eerdmans Publishing Company, 1982), 484-490.

10. From an unpublished account of a soldier attending the infantry school at Fort Benning, Ga. in October 1988.

11. *Dictionary of Contemporary Quotations*, 3rd edition. Edited by John Gordon Burke and Ned Kehde. (N.p.: John Gordon Burke Publisher, 1994), 95.

12. W. E. Vine, Merrill F. Unger, and William White, *An Expository Dictionary of Biblical Words* (Nashville: Thomas Nelson Publishers, 1984), 992. J. D. Douglas et al., *The*

New Bible Dictionary (Grand Rapids: Wm. B. Eerdmans Publishing Company, 1975), 1145.

13. John Sandford and Mark Sandford, *A Comprehensive Guide to Deliverance and Inner Healing*, (Grand Rapids: Chosen Books, a Division of Baker Book House Company, 1992), 44. Used with permission.

14. Gary Kinnaman, *Angels Dark and Light*, (Ann Arbor, Mich.: Servant Publications, 1994), 148. Used with permission.

15. Anne Graham Lotz, *The Vision of His Glory* (Nashville: Word Publishing, 1997), 130-131. Used with permission.

16. Testimony by John Sandford, June 1999. Used with permission.

17. *The New Bible Dictionary* (Grand Rapids: Wm. B. Eerdmans Publishing Co., 1975), 153.

18. Testimony by John Sandford, February 26, 1999. Used with permission.

19. Taken from *The Secret Place*, a message Graham Cooke gave at Toronto Airport Christian Fellowship on June 2, 1996.

20. John Sandford and Mark Sandford, *A Comprehensive Guide to Deliverance and Inner Healing*, (Grand Rapids: Chosen Books, a Division of Baker Book House Company, 1992), 276. Used with permission.

Recommended Reading

Anderson, Neil T. *The Bondage Breaker*. Eugene, Oreg.: Harvest House Publishers, 1990.

— *Released From Bondage*. Nashville, Tenn.: Thomas Nelson, Inc., 1993.

— *Victory Over Darkness*. Ventura, Calif.: Regal Books, 1990.

Bounds, E. M. *Winning the Invisible War*. Springfield, Pa.: Whitaker House, 1984.

Chevreau, Guy. *Pray With Fire: Interceding in the Spirit*. New York: HarperCollins, 1995.

Cornwall, Judson. *It's God's War: A Biblical View of Spiritual Warfare*. Hagerstown, Md.: McDougal Publishing, 1998.

Dake, Finis. *Heavenly Hosts: A Biblical Study of Angels*. Dake Publishing, 1995.

Devenish, David. *Demolishing Strongholds: Effective Strategies for Spiritual Warfare*. Milton Keynes, England: Word Publishing, 2000.

Engle, Lou. *Digging the Wells of Revival: Reclaiming Your Historic Inheritance Through Prophetic Intercession*. Shippensburg, Pa.: Revival Press, 1998.

Forsyth, P.T., *The Soul of Prayer*. Salem, Ohio: Schmul Publishing Co., Inc., 1986.

Foster, Richard J. *Prayer: Finding the Heart's True Home.* San Francisco: HarperSan Francisco a division of Harper Collins Publishers, 1992.

Gibson, Noel and Phyl. *Deliver Our Children From the Evil One.* Kent, U.K.: Sovereign World, Ltd., 1992.

— *Evicting Demonic Intruders.* Chichester, U.K.: New Wine Press, 1993.

Goll, Jim W. *The Lost Art of Intercession.* Shippensburg, Pa.: Revival Press, 1998.

Kinnaman, Gary. *Angels: Dark and Light.* Ann Arbor, Mich.: Servant Publications, 1994.

Lake, John G. *Adventures in God.* Tulsa: Harrison House, 1981.

Larkin, Clarence. *The Spirit World.* Glenside, Pa.: Clarence Larkin Ministries, 1921.

Law, Terry. *The Truth About Angels.* Lake Mary, Fla.: Creation House, 1994.

Lloyd-Jones, D. Martin. *The Christian Warfare: An Exposition of Ephesians 6:10-13.* Grand Rapids: Baker Book House, 1976.

McGaw, Francis. *John Hyde: The Apostle of Prayer.* Minneapolis: Bethany House Publishers, 1970.

Michaelson, Johnanna. *The Beautiful Side of Evil.* Eugene, Oreg.: Harvest House Publishers, 1982.

Mira, Greg. *Victor or Victim.* Grandview, Mo.: Grace! Publishing Company, 1992.

Payne, Leanne. *Listening Prayer: Learning to Hear God's Voice and Keep a Prayer Journal.* Grand Rapids: Baker Books House, 1994.

Penn-Lewis, Jesse. *War On The Saints*. New York: Thomas E. Lowe, Ltd., 1986.

Pittman, Howard O. *The Covert War*. Foxworth, Miss.: Howard Pittman Ministries, n.d.

— *The Day Star*. Foxworth, Miss.: Howard Pittman Ministries, n.d.

— *The Curse*. Foxworth, Miss.: Howard Pittman Ministries, 1988.

— *Placebo*. Foxworth, Miss.: Howard Pittman Ministries, n.d.

— *Demons: An Eyewitness Account*. Foxworth, Miss.: Howard Pittman Ministries, n.d.

Ryle, J.C. *The Complete Armour: A Treatise of the Saint's War Against the Devil*. Suffolk, U.K.: Richard Clay Ltd., 1987.

Sandford, John, and Mark Sandford. *A Comprehensive Guide to Deliverance and Inner Healing*. Grand Rapids: Chosen Books, 1992.

Sandford, John, and R. Loren Sandford. *The Renewal of the Mind*. Tulsa: Victory House Publishers, 1991.

Sandford, John Loren. *Healing the Nations*. Grand Rapids: Chosen Books, a Division of Baker Book House Company, 2000.

Smith, Alice. *Beyond the Veil: Entering Into Intimacy with God through Prayer*. Ventura, Calif.: Regal Books, 1997.

Stratford, Lauren. *Satan's Underground: The Extraordinary Story of One Woman's Escape*. Eugene, Oreg.: Harvest House Publishers, 1988.

Torrey, R.A. *How to Pray*. New Kensington, Pa.: Whitaker House, 1983.

Unger, Merrill F. *Demons in the World Today*. Wheaton, Ill.: Tyndale House Publishers, Inc., 1984.

White, John. *The Fight*. Downers Grove, Ill.: InterVarsity Press, 1976.

About the Author

JOHN PAUL JACKSON is a husband, father, and established authority on Christian spirituality and dream interpretation. His Biblical approach to dreams reveals their life-changing purpose, and restores an overlooked way God chooses to communicate with people.

John Paul's teachings have stirred and renewed passion for God among people of all ages from various faith backgrounds. His thoughtful "explanations of the unexplainable" and simple, yet profound, concepts help people relate to God and each other in fresh ways.

As an author, speaker, and television guest, John Paul has impacted hundreds of thousands of people, emphasizing character as a key element in the true spiritual life. His many years of study and experience have made him a respected and sought-after spiritual advisor to leaders and believers around the world.

John Paul has shared his practical and spiritual expertise with an international audience through the Streams Training Center courses and publications.

I AM: 365 NAMES OF GOD
By John Paul Jackson
Designed for daily reading and meditation, this collection of
365 names of God will guide you into becoming a person who
consistently abides in God's presence. Hardback.

RETAIL $15

I AM: INHERITING THE FULLNESS OF GOD'S NAMES
By John Paul Jackson
As you embark on the glorious adventure of knowing God,
let Him show you the amazing mysteries and wonders
revealed for those who bear His name.

RETAIL $10

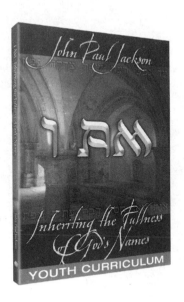

I AM: 365 NAMES OF GOD
YOUTH CURRICULUM
By John Paul Jackson and Jordan Bateman

A life-changing resource, the *I AM Youth Curriculum* offers twelve powerful lessons on the names of God. It includes a teacher's guide and reproducible student materials, so no separate student books are needed. Filled with relevant activities, skits, and teacher tips, it's ideal for youth groups, Sunday school, Bible studies, homeschools, and small groups.

RETAIL $15

I AM: 365 NAMES OF GOD CD

Listen as author John Paul Jackson reads the names of God to music composed by Graham Ord. Experience the peace, comfort, healing, provision, and transforming power that come from meditating on God's names.

RETAIL $16

BREATH OF I AM CD

Ideal for times of meditation, prayer, and therapeutic healing, this soothing instrumental sound track to the *I AM* CD creates an atmosphere that will soothe your spirit and calm your soul.

RETAIL $16

BREAKING FREE OF REJECTION
By John Paul Jackson

In this compassionate and spiritually insightful book, John Paul Jackson explains what happens when rejection rules our lives. Discover how to harness the power of rejection, dramatically improve your life, and walk into the extraordinary quality of life God desires for you.

RETAIL $10

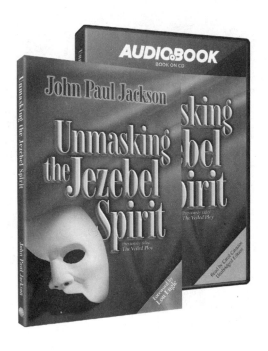

UNMASKING THE JEZEBEL SPIRIT
By John Paul Jackson

With keen insight, John Paul Jackson peers through the enemy's smoke screen and exposes one of the most deceptive snares used to destroy the Church. This fascinating book is biblically anchored and seasoned with years of divine revelation and thoughtful reflection.

Also available as an AudioBook.

RETAIL $13

AUDIOBOOK RETAIL $16

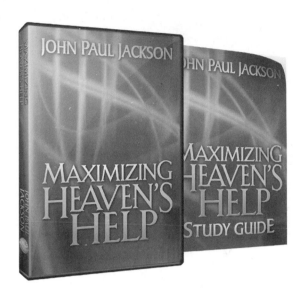

Maximizing Heaven's Help (Set)
John Paul Jackson

Understand how to activate God's angels in your life. Discover how to change destructive cycles. Learn how to position yourself to unleash your full potential.
Includes: 4-CD Teaching Set and Study Guide

Retail $32

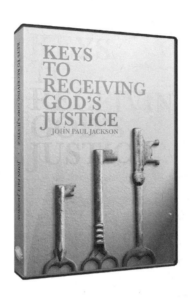

KEYS TO RECEIVING GOD'S JUSTICE
John Paul Jackson

Have you been attacked, robbed, or cheated by the enemy?
Implement God's plan of justice in your life to avenge the
enemy's attacks. Insure that you and your family receive every
blessing stolen from your generational line.
One DVD and One CD

RETAIL $24

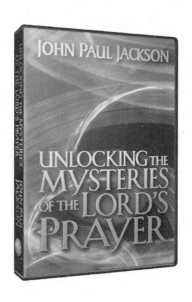

Unlocking the Mysteries of the Lord's Prayer
John Paul Jackson

Are you hungry for a deeper revelation of prayer? Uncover
seven dimensions of the Lord's prayer and grasp essential keys
that open the doors of Heaven.
4-CD Set

Retail $27

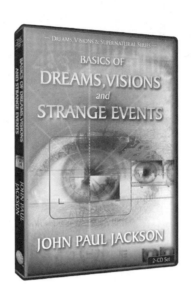

BASICS OF DREAMS, VISIONS, AND STRANGE EVENTS
John Paul Jackson

Take the first steps toward understanding your dreams!
Unravel the difference between God speaking and making
Himself known. Reflect on biblical imagery in dreams and
discover how to change the outcome of a dream. Learn why
you can't interpret a dream with a secular dream dictionary.
2-CD Set

RETAIL $17

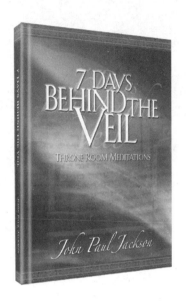

7 Days Behind the Veil
John Paul Jackson

What would it take for you to embark on a journey of the heart? This type of journey doesn't allow for a religious spirit, and only one thing is certain: You will never be the same again. Join John Paul Jackson as he describes what it is like to love God from Heaven's throne room, touching what you've only dreamed about-and suddenly discovering that your dreams were far too small.

Retail $10

STREAMS INSTITUTE FOR SPIRITUAL DEVELOPMENT

John Paul Jackson, Founder

At Streams, we seek to give shape to ideas that educate, inform, and cause people to better understand and delight in God. We endeavor to enrich people's lives by satisfying their lifelong need to identify and use their God-given gifts. We seek to be used by God to heal, renew, and encourage pastors and church leaders.

COURSES OFFERED INCLUDE:

Course 101: The Art of Hearing God
Course 102: Advanced Prophetic Ministry
Course 201: Understanding Dreams and Visions
Course 202: Advanced Workshop in Dream Interpretation
Course 301: Living the Spiritual Life

More information is available online at
www.streamsministries.com or by calling 1.888.441.8080.

Order Form

- ORDER ONLINE: www.streamsministries.com
- CALL TOLL-FREE (U.S. AND CANADA): **1.888.441.8080**
- POSTAL ORDERS: **Streams Ministries, 1420 Lakeside Pkwy. Suite 100
Flower Mound, TX 75028, USA**

QUANTITY	TITLE	PRICE
_____	_____	_____
_____	_____	_____
_____	_____	_____
_____	_____	_____

DOMESTIC SHIPPING AND HANDLING CHARGES   SUBTOTAL _____

Up to $20 $5.00   SHIPPING AND HANDLING _____

$20.01 to $50.00 $7.00   TOTAL _____

$50.01 to $75.00 $8.00

$75.01 to $100.00 $9.00

More than $100   10% of Subtotal

For AK, HI, PR, USVI, Canada, or Mexico, please double the shipping charges.

INTERNATIONAL RATES: All international orders must be paid by credit card only.

Please specify international surface or airmail shipping. The shipping cost will be added to your

credit card charges.

(PLEASE PRINT CLEARLY)

NAME: _____

STREET ADDRESS: _____

APT. _____ CITY: _____

STATE: _____ ZIP: _____

COUNTRY: _____ PHONE: _____

E-MAIL: _____

METHOD OF PAYMENT:

___ Check or Money Order (Make check payable to *Streams Ministries)*

___ Credit Card: ❑ Visa ❑ MasterCard ❑ American Express ❑ Discover

CARD NUMBER: _____-_____-_____-_____ EXPIRATION DATE:____/_____

CARD HOLDER (please print):_____

SIGNATURE : _____

(Credit card orders cannot be processed without signature.)